Praise for *Touch th*

"A wise, thoughtful book engaging in ⸻ and magic, reason, and intuition … D⸻ ⸻⸺⸻ powerful teachings, concepts, and discussions into something that can be easily understood and put to use."

—Christopher Penczak, author of *The Inner Temple of Witchcraft*

"*Touch the Earth, Kiss the Sky* presents animism through the seasons at its most applicable and actionable."

—S. Kelley Harrell, M.Div., author of *Runic Book of Days*

"This book is a gold mine of wisdom, intelligence, and insight. Coaching the reader through fantastic exercises and practices, *Touch the Earth, Kiss the Sky* is sure to enhance any reader's connection and understanding of the mysteries through direct experience."

—Mat Auryn, author of *Psychic Witch*

"Discussions of the intersection of science and magic are intellectually engaging. The suggested practices for aligning with the eight-fold Wheel of the Year are deeply satisfying. I especially appreciate both the 'touch the earth' sections—outer, practical practices—and the 'kiss the sky' sections—inner practices."

—Joanna Powell Colbert, creator of the *Gaian Tarot*

"Diotima is both a broad and a deep thinker and her years of experience as a soil scientist, astrologer, and priestess are evident in this stunning book."

—Byron Ballard, author of *Earth Works*

"Diotima has done a remarkable job opening the middle path and interconnection between the scientist and the mystic. In *Touch the Earth, Kiss the Sky* one will find a treasure house of resources, information, and guidance."

—Aeptha Jennette, high priestess and
ceremonialist with Light Haven

"An accessible and beautifully written bridge between consensual material reality and the realms of Greater Consciousness."

—Karel James Bouse, Ph.D., author of
Neo-shamanism and Mental Health

"The perfect book for the smart rationalist that has a magic-shaped hole in their soul. Diotima speaks directly to the beginner that perhaps has doubts about magic, while also engaging the experienced reader in views and methods that they perhaps never considered before."

—Jason Miller, author of *Elements of Spellcrafting*

"*Touch the Earth, Kiss the Sky* gives you the ideas, insights, and techniques to find your own way into an expanded reality filled with starry wonder and rooted deeply in the soil…It is a book that is meant to be read slowly and savored. If you do the work described in *Touch the Earth, Kiss the Sky*, you will be changed."

—Ivo Dominguez, Jr., author of *Keys to Perception*

"With insightful philosophy, models of science, magical theory, Pagan and indigenous wisdom, and useful exercises, Diotima inspires and invites us to walk the spiritual and magical path with practical feet, developing ourselves at the crossroads of science and spirituality."

—Orion Foxwood, author of *The Tree of Enchantment*

"Diotima has created a book on pagan spirituality truly for the modern age. It successfully integrates modern Quantum Theory with magic and spirituality without any dichotomy in theory. We'd highly recommend it for both beginners and seasoned practitioners."

—Janet Farrar and Gavin Bone, authors of *A Witches' Bible*

"Generously filled with wonderful reference material and written by a woman who is both a scientist and a gifted witch, this book provides dozens of ways for scientists to experiment with magic and for magic workers to understand some of the science behind what they do."

—Hecate Demetersdatter, witch and blogger
at hecatedemeter.wordpress.com

TOUCH THE
EARTH
KISS THE SKY

About the Author

Diotima Mantineia (Asheville, NC) is a practicing witch and has been a professional astrologer and tarot reader for more than twenty-five years. She writes for *Witches & Pagans* and teaches widely. Her passion for science led her to a degree in soil and crop science as well as graduate work in the field.

DIOTIMA MANTINEIA

TOUCH THE
EARTH
KISS THE SKY

Allowing the Rational Mind to
Welcome Magic & Spirituality

Llewellyn Publications
Woodbury, Minnesota

FIRST EDITION
First Printing, 2020

Book design by Samantha Penn
Cover design by Shannon McKuhen
Editing by Brian Erdrich
Interior art by the Llewellyn Art Department

Llewellyn Publications is a registered trademark of Llewellyn Worldwide Ltd.

Library of Congress Cataloging-in-Publication Data (Pending)
ISBN: 978-0-7387-6134-3

Llewellyn Publications
A Division of Llewellyn Worldwide Ltd.
2143 Wooddale Drive
Woodbury, MN 55125-2989
www.llewellyn.com

Printed in the United States of America

To all my Teachers

Contents

Contents

Introduction

If you have often found yourself torn between science and spirituality, if you've felt a holy and sacred connection to the stars, to Earth, to Nature's soaring creations but not followed your heart into a deeper psychic, poetic connection because you feared you might have to sacrifice your rationality, then I've written this book for you.

If you sense a depth and brilliance to life that is often veiled as you navigate your way through your daily routines in consensus reality and you want to explore that depth, to tear the veil away, but you don't quite know how to go about doing that, then I've written this book for you.

If you've always been deeply curious about the workings of this world and think science is one of the coolest creations of the human race but the materialist conclusions of scientific orthodoxy depress you, then I've written this book for you.

You may already follow a particular religion or spiritual tradition but don't feel that it really fits you. Maybe it puts religious orthodoxy over science, and that just doesn't seem right to you. Maybe you don't get any real sense of inspiration or connection from it, or perhaps its precepts don't really agree with your own ideas but it gives you a spiritual community, so you stick with it anyway.

Or perhaps you have no defined spiritual path or acknowledged religion at all, though you feel the lack of some kind of higher guidance in your life. Perhaps you're not really sure what you believe. You may have imagined going off on a retreat to think about these things and get clear on it all—someday.

"Someday," however, is usually a little white lie you tell yourself because there always seems to be something else to spend the time and/or money on. But you don't need to sit in a cave in India, go on a vision quest in the forest, find shamans in Peru, or meditate on the patio of a luxury "spiritual resort" to map a path ahead that leads to fulfilling your soul's vision for this lifetime. Nor do you need to abandon rational, logical thought to pursue spiritual goals. You can map out your own path, your unique, creative engagement with reality and the universe itself, by simply committing some time to a considered sequence of thought and practice that fits within the demands of your daily life.

My work as an astrologer—learning about people's dreams and visions, their challenges and sorrows, their soul-level longings—has made me very aware of how many people are conflicted and uncertain about their spiritual beliefs. This is unsurprising, since the high priests of our cultural religion, science, mostly deny that there *is* any spiritual reality or consciousness outside of the confines of physical reality, while the high priests of the majority religions mostly say there's only one true way—theirs, of course. But my own experiences and my conversations with others have convinced me that we all have a timeless and vibrant existence outside of physical reality—a soul, in other words—and we come into this world of time and space "trailing clouds of glory," with a plan for that soul to create, grow, and expand its awareness.

I've spent a considerable amount of time studying science, both formally, in college and grad school, and informally, through reading and classes. I think it's one of the most remarkable and useful inventions of the human mind—even though we do tend to make a religion out of it in direct contravention of its own tenets. I've also been actively pursuing my own spiritual journey for well over half a century. I've managed to learn a few things as I stumbled along, looking for and finding a synthesis of science and spirituality that makes sense to me.

So I can say with some certainty that to explore the sacred connections you sense, to expand your awareness into the realm of spirit requires only your curiosity and a determination to follow where reason, experience, intuition, and results lead you. There are things you'll need to spend some time thinking about and things you'll need to actually do. (Experience is important.) This book offers some fruitful lines of intellectual investigation, some experiential and spiritual practices, and a framework for a year of spiritual study and exploration woven around the cycles of the Sun and natural seasonal changes. Hopefully, by the end of the year you will have begun to uncover an intellectually and emotionally satisfying way of approaching your daily life with a greater spiritual awareness and a greater sense of joy and fulfillment.

This is also a book about magic—about influencing and changing the physical world through subtle energies of Consciousness and connection. We'll look at both the theory and practice of magic as well as how it changes us and the world around us.

Personally, I structure my spiritual life around a path that might be described as "Eclectic Wicca." Wicca's basic structure of the seasons—the Sabbats, the Wheel of the Year—define my spiritual year, and I still work with many of Wicca's symbols, myths, and magical techniques, though the many other magical systems, philosophies, and religions I've studied are incorporated into my path as well. Fortunately, Wicca's underlying structure is flexible enough to allow for this.

But this is not a book about Wicca. After investigating a number of Earth-based religions that fall under the umbrella of modern Paganism, inquiring into most of the world's great religions and exploring some of them in depth, studying under teachers in indigenous and modern shamanic traditions, learning magic from talented magicians, books, and personal experience, the conclusion I have come to is that each one of us must find our own way through the Great Mystery—the origins and meaning of life.

Discovering our own way involves work we must do to determine our personal answers to the eternal question of "How should I live?" It involves work we must do in order to learn to use the power of our free will, to come to full awareness of our soul's plan for this lifetime, to create change within this shared reality of time and space. It involves facing our earthly lives head on, with courage, gratitude, curiosity, an open heart, and a willingness to create change as we make the daily choices that form our lives.

This is what our search for a spiritual path boils down to. What we do, what we say, even what we think—these are choices we make, every hour of every day. If we do not want our choices to be driven by unconscious, karmic forces, we need to create an intellectual and spiritual foundation on which we build our lives so that we create and choose consciously.

People follow a particular religion or spiritual path for a variety of reasons—usually because they hope to find happiness (or at least contentment), discover meaning that helps them make sense of the difficult events, and/or gain protection from whatever they fear. Perhaps they were told as children what God is, what path He wants them to follow. (And it's usually "He"—male and capitalized—because, like The Highlander, there can be only one.) It's easy to internalize a path taught in childhood and follow it because "that's the way things are." But finding your true spiritual path is not a question of placating a vengeful deity or deities or conforming to certain laws or simply having "faith."

- Finding your spiritual path means learning to carefully observe yourself, others, and the world around you. It means training your mind to be both strong and flexible. Once you have certain habits of observation and thinking in place, you can live with much greater clarity and insight.

- Finding your spiritual path means making conscious decisions about how the world works and how you want to live in it based on your own research, personal insights, and creative inclinations. Once certain basic decisions are made and values established, making daily decisions becomes easier.

- Finding your spiritual path means exploring your emotions and your unconscious. Once we learn that our emotions are engines of creativity that can be harnessed and directed, we discover how to expand into joy and deep connection with others, Nature, the cosmos, and Consciousness. (I'll explain why Consciousness is capitalized in chapter 2.)

- Finding your spiritual path means creating a practice for yourself—some combination of meditation, contemplation, prayer, trancework, celebration, ritual, breathwork and physical exercise—that keeps you focused, aware, and on track to your personal spiritual and life goals.

Our soul naturally seeks growth and change. No baby can stay a baby. No child can stay a child. No adult can avoid aging. We can't stop our souls from growing and changing any more than we can stop our bodies from growing and changing. What we can do is offer our soul the same things we (hopefully) offer our children—nourishment, education, and habits of mind and body that lead to health and optimal development. If we don't give our souls what they need, we can stunt their growth in the same way a child's physical, mental, and emotional growth can be stunted through neglect or abuse.

It's not only our own lives that change as we do. Every person who takes conscious charge of their soul's growth changes their personal resonance, the vibration that emanates from them. We all have a personal vibration that affects every person we interact with. Changing ourselves is always the first step in changing the world.

As an astrologer, I look at long-term cycles through the immutable patterns of the planets. As a Witch, I live my life intensely aware of and deeply connected to the cycles of Nature. I spent a number of years training to be a scientist, so I've learned to investigate the ways and the nature of physical reality. I also am—first and always—a seeker, someone who consciously walks a path that leads into the Great Mystery.

I'm writing this book to offer whatever benefit my half-century or so of active seeking might hold for you. Too many of my younger years were spent stumbling around in the world, down dead ends and back out again. I eventually found my way through a healing, transformative labyrinth that has led me to a solid, core awareness of spirit and a life I love. While I was fortunate enough to have many excellent teachers, I know that if I had been offered better guidance when I was younger, I would have found my way much sooner. So I've pulled together what I see as some of the most important discoveries on my journey in the hopes of helping you map out your own path.

Finding and defining your own spiritual path will take work, though perhaps not as much time as you think. The work will, unquestionably, change your life. I'll give you some of my thoughts on spirituality and magic, and introduce you to tools, techniques, and rituals that have dramatically changed my life for the better by broadening my awareness of spiritual realities. I hope that this information will help you find your own way to a clear connection with spirit and a path that you can walk in confidence that you are heading in the right direction—the right direction for you.

Cultural Questions

Since we'll be exploring magical techniques and spiritual tools that are used by many different cultures, lets detour here for a brief discussion of cultural appropriation. There's a lot of (often heated) discussion about it online, and definitions differ. I'd define it as the careless adoption—usually unacknowledged and/or unapproved—of the symbols, rituals, customs, and practices of one culture by the people of another, usually more dominant culture.

Cultural appropriation is a sensitive issue, and rightly so. It can get even stickier when there is disagreement within the group whose culture is being copied as to what is and is not cultural appropriation. You probably recognize the power imbalances that are at the heart of this discussion. For instance, Native Americans had many thriving cultures throughout the length and breadth of what we now call the United States of America. Most of those cultures were deliberately destroyed, first by various European groups, and finally by the government of the USA, who repeatedly dealt in bad faith, breaking treaties, contracts, and deliberately committing cultural and physical genocide. Native American people were herded onto reservations and had their ancestral cultures actively, sometimes violently, repressed.

Another example is the African-American culture created by people who had been enslaved and brought to this country from Africa. Like the Native Americans, they have been subjected to deeply racist laws and attitudes, offensive stereotypes, and social and financial injustice. Their many important contributions to our modern culture often go unacknowledged.

Many people feel these groups have every right to deny white people the use of their cultural items and practices, such as sweat lodges or dreadlocks, musical items such as Native American flutes, hip-hop and rap, or the improper use of words associated with that group. For instance, "ghetto" is not (or should not be) a fashion description. That usage can be offensive to both Black people and Jews because it makes light of the pain and suffering experienced by those groups in actual ghettos.

On the other hand, it's undeniable that humans have been cross-pollinating each other's cultures for as long as we've had culture. There's nothing wrong with adopting aspects of another culture if it's done with respect and clear communication. But all too frequently, it is not. This is not the place for a deep discussion of the issue, but it's one you will almost certainly run across in your spiritual explorations. Because your actions vis-à-vis this topic will affect others, your careful thought and attention to the issue is necessary. Here are some of my thoughts about it you may find of help.

The first thing I look at if I'm considering working with a tool or technique from a different culture is the willingness to share. There is no need for me to adopt the practices of a culture that is marginalized and struggling to maintain their identity and that has specifically said they do not want others using those tools or practices.

On the other hand, the principles and practices of, for instance, Yoga and Chinese martial arts have been actively and widely shared by representatives of those thriving cultures for well over a century. I've studied and practiced Yoga since I was nineteen—over forty-five years ago as I write this—and spent many years studying and practicing Chinese martial arts. I did both at schools that were founded by native practitioners of those disciplines who came to America eager to share their knowledge.

I was taught ways of magic, divination, and ancestor honoring by Malidoma Somé, a tribal elder of the Dagara tribe of West Africa who teaches internationally with the encouragement of other elders of the tribe. I learned spiritual/ magical techniques and the cultural framework of the Peruvian Q'ero from Peruvian paqos (spiritual healers/shamans/mystics) and American teachers who had themselves learned directly from Peruvian paqos.

All that knowledge has considerably enriched my spiritual understanding and practice, and I am grateful for it. I do not consider my use of the tools and techniques I have learned from these studies to be cultural appropriation since they were freely shared, and I have not taken more from those cultures than was offered. But I've also found that, having learned them, I don't use many of them because the cultural framework is not my own and the spirits they work with are often deeply tied to their land, but not mine. What has happened is that I've noted parallels between techniques of the magical traditions and philosophies I practice, which are mostly sourced in Western Europe, and theirs. Then I've used that knowledge to help me fill in some blanks that were left in the magical traditions of pagan Europe due to the cultural and actual genocide perpetrated by the Christian church in its quest to eliminate paganism.

Humans like to share with each other. It's a natural impulse and a beneficial one. I see no reason to set up artificial barriers by declaring cultural appropriation when the culture itself is not marginalized and/or people of the culture in question are the ones teaching it. I find these artificial barriers particularly problematic if the person declaring something to be appropriation is from a different culture entirely, which happens all too often.

It gets stickier, of course, when there is a great deal of disagreement within the culture in question over what is and is not appropriate to share, as is often the case with Native American cultures. There are two considerations here. First, are we talking about technology, or are we talking about culture-specific spirits and prayers?

For instance, building a dome-shaped hut with local materials and sitting in it with hot rocks and water by itself is not cultural appropriation. It's simply a wise use of local materials to do something that has been done across cultures and time—sit in a small enclosure and generate steam through hot stones for reasons of physical and spiritual health. Some things, like the line of energy between the fire that heats the rocks and the rocks in the center of the hut, which many Native Americans believe is a line that should never be stepped across, is easily perceived by sensitive people, no matter their lineage. This is not a question of culture, it's a question of perception of natural forces. But if you use Native American language, call it a "sweat lodge," begin with a "pipe ceremony," and call on Native American spirits, then you are walking a thin line that may well cross the line into appropriation, depending on your training and connection to the culture involved.

This brings us to the second consideration, which is one's level of knowledge and respect regarding this culture. How connected are you with the culture whose rituals you are using? How much have you studied it—both its history and current conditions? How many people in that culture do you know? If it is a marginalized culture, how are you helping the people who are the modern carriers of that culture? How are you giving back to that culture? Were you taught this ceremony by a member of the culture and given permission to use it or are you just grabbing onto what you've read in books?

Some soul-searching is in order here. What draws you to the practices and ideas of this culture? Are you sensing a deep past life connection or have you just met some people who are into it and it seems cool? If you sense a deep connection, then you begin by connecting with the people who hold the lineage of that culture today because they were born into it and have an ancestral connection to it. If you cannot find a way to be accepted by the people, if they are unwilling to share their practices with you and you have no direct ancestral connection to it, then find another way of expressing your spiritual longings. Even if you have clear memories of a past life in that culture, you were not born into it in this life. There's probably a reason for that.

How to Use This Book

I'll start this section by explaining some of my nonstandard grammatical choices when it comes to capitalization, so you know what I mean when I refer to Fire instead of fire, Nature instead of nature, or the Web of Life instead of the web of life. While I admittedly read a lot of Winnie the Pooh books as a child and recall a previous lifetime in the eighteenth century, back when Random Capitalization was all the rage, the real reason for the capitalization is that I'm an animist. That means I believe there are overlighting intelligences that direct the physical manifestations of life on our planet, and those intelligences are what I'm referring to when I capitalize Nature or Fire. (You'll learn more about animism in chapter 11 and the four classical elements in chapter 13.)

A big part of this book's value is in the resources sections at the end of the chapters. To keep the book from becoming a tome, I've given only a brief introduction to the topics I'm covering and a few basic exercises. Then it's up to you and your intuitive sense of what's right for you to choose which topics you want to explore in more depth and in which order.

I've organized the book around the eight divisions of the year that are the scaffolding of quite a few modern Pagan traditions—the Sabbats, which together comprise the Wheel of the Year. But we are going to look at the Wheel of the Year from a more scientific standpoint. These divisions mark actual astronomical events—the Sun reaching the points of the solstices and equinoxes and the midpoints between them—and so make an excellent framework upon which you can build your own liturgical calendar as you explore, discover, and develop your personal spirituality. You don't need to call them Sabbats or use the Pagan names for them (though you certainly can, and I'll include them). In this book, I call them Stations of the Sun because they mark off sections of the ecliptic—the apparent path of the Sun around Earth. The sections on each Station will help you develop holiday celebrations that are tailored to your beliefs and the ecosystem in which you live.

For each Station, we'll "touch the earth"—ground ourselves by establishing daily habits, taking certain actions, and performing intentional ritual to tune our bodies and minds to the changing seasons. We'll explore practical, physical ways to enhance our ability to create change in the world. At each Station, we'll also "kiss the sky"—intellectually considering the meaning of the seasonal shifts, exploring personal beliefs and values, and expanding our awareness and understanding of the universe through study and contemplation.

As you work through the Wheel of the Year, you'll clarify what you believe, determine what you really want and why you want it, and enhance your personal power—your ability to act effectively in the world. A word of warning—you'll also encounter obstacles within yourself and in your life that will slow you down, make you stumble, and fan all your fears. This work is not easy. It requires courage, persistence, and a willingness to change. But the rewards include joy, a stronger sense of connection to a larger reality, and the return of your sense of wonder. You reap those rewards by breaking through, facing fears, moving in the direction you need to go. Persistence is the key.

A Spirituality of Nature

The Touch the Earth sections will also feature ways of connecting with the Web of Life on this planet, respecting and understanding how Nature works. I don't think spirituality can be separated from our physical existence, and I firmly believe that connecting with Nature is not only the quickest and clearest way to a deeper understanding of the Universe, but the surest path to claiming our power and creative abilities within it.

You'll learn about and experience the etheric energies that underlie physical reality. We'll explore various techniques to help you connect with the spirits of your land and your personal helping spirits. We'll look at how to live a magical life, weaving Earth energies into our daily lives and becoming more aware of how we affect the Web of Life through our myriad daily choices.

The Kiss the Sky sections involve building the intellectual and emotional framework of your life, exploring what you really believe, what your core values are, and the nature of your own self—what makes you the individual that you are. You'll learn about the natural world around you and also do deep, personal psychological work, developing a greater awareness of your emotions and unconscious while excavating things like conflicting beliefs established in childhood (or past lives) that cause us to self-sabotage. We'll also explore the whys and wherefores of interacting with beings who are nonphysical, from ghosts to ancestors to helping spirits to deities both ancient and modern.

We humans are not the entirely rational creatures we like to suppose we are because (to paraphrase Walt Whitman) we are large and contain multitudes. It's impossible to hold the totality of our existence within the framework of our conscious awareness in physical reality, in time and space. So we must learn to expand our awareness into our Greater Self—a term I prefer to indicate what many call the Higher Self. It's important to work with and train that rational mind, but not let ourselves be confined by it. We must remain open to the reality of things we may not be able to fully understand from our limited perspective.

I suggest reading the book through once and then starting the practices wherever you are on the Wheel of the Year as you read it or in whatever order feels right to you. Acquire a journal and get in the habit of using it. Make notes, as you go through the book, about what interests you and what you want to explore further.

You might also want to get a notebook to keep various papers of interest you will accumulate and to make useful notes on seasonal rituals, meditations, and magical insights. (Keep these separate from your journal because you'll want to refer to them frequently and change them around.)

You must do the work. Read the books, do the meditation, perform the rituals, plant the garden, walk in the woods, seize the day. Let yourself be a child at play. Feel the curiosity within you, nurture it, and let it grow. Give your creative self an outlet. Try something different. See where it leads.

I'll do my best to lay down a path through New Age wildernesses, swamps of religious dogma, and mazes of scientific obfuscation that will lead you to the mystic's wild garden. Here, you can sit, think, and figure things out for yourself. Here, you can decide how you want to live, what makes sense to you, and why. Here, you can connect with the larger reality of which you are a part.

Let's get started.

CHAPTER ONE
Stations of the Sun

If we want to create a coherent, useful, Nature-connected spiritual path, it's important to have regular holidays (holy days)—dates set aside for celebration and deliberate, conscious reconnection with the Divine. Days during which we can reconnect with our own sacred vision of the world, as well as our spiritual guides and fellow seekers.

Some ancient cultures celebrated solstices and/or equinoxes, and some—most notably Celtic cultures—observed what we refer to as the "cross-quarters," traditional dates that are roughly at the midpoints between solstice and equinox, equinox and solstice. These holidays were celebrated in various ways in various cultures, usually within just a few days of the exact midpoints. The various traditional cultural rituals are fascinating and worth studying. (Did you know, for instance, that the Halloween jack-o'-lantern is an American adaptation of an Irish Samhain custom?) But you needn't try to recreate these rituals.

The modern Pagan revival, especially in its Wiccan incarnation, brought the Celtic fire festivals and the solstices and equinoxes together in a yearly, eight-part series of rituals celebrating the apparent path of the Sun around Earth, and they have become known in our culture as the eight Sabbats. The eight Wiccan Sabbats are not known to have been celebrated together in any one religion or culture before Gerald Gardner's inspired, mid-twentieth century invention/reimagining of an Earth-based, God/dess-worshiping religion. Gardner plucked what he could from the available history and then invented the rest. But these dates reflect actual astronomical events; they are not exclusively Wiccan.

These Stations of the Sun offer a reason for ritual and celebration, which humans crave, even when our cultural or religious background denies them. The need for ritual seems to be hardwired into our neurobiology, and when done thoughtfully and consciously, rituals and celebrations improve our lives and strengthen our communities.

There are solid astronomical and astrological reasons for celebrating and working magic on these eight Stations of the Sun. Whether you consider our star to be nothing more than a ball of plasma in a purely material world or believe it is an intelligent being in its own right—a deity of some kind, or simply a planetary intelligence—there is no question that the Sun is of primary importance to our life here on Earth. Marking its passages through various Stations on the ecliptic (the apparent path of the Sun around Earth) is a perfectly natural and practical way of marking the change of seasons.

An understanding of the astronomy and some insights from the astrology will help you use these holidays to anchor your own personal spiritual practice. But if you aren't interested in the technical details, feel free to skip over them. The meaning is more important than the mechanics. The main takeaway is that the eight Stations of the Sun are simply points on the circle of the Sun's apparent path around the Earth: the solstices, equinoxes, and the midpoints between them.

I'll describe the astronomy of what's actually going on in the sky while we're celebrating Sabbats, but I'm going to do it from an astrological perspective. Did you know that the tropical zodiac of astrology is an accurate celestial coordinate system? That may surprise you. Astrologers are frequently accused of not even understanding basic astronomy, particularly the precession of the equinoxes, and here I am saying that our charts are accurate maps of the placement of the planets and other objects. But they are, which means we can use the signs and degrees of the zodiac to accurately place the Sun's current position on the ecliptic.

But now, back to the astronomy. A celestial coordinate system must have a fundamental plane as its baseline, and the zodiac uses the plane of the ecliptic, the circle of the apparent path of the Sun around Earth. To be precise, the zodiac is what astronomers refer to as a "geocentric ecliptic coordinate system," which uses the point of the Spring Equinox as the beginning and ending point of the ecliptic circle. Western astrologers call this point 0 degrees of the sign of Aries. The 360 degrees of the ecliptic are then divided into equal slices of 30 degrees each, and these divisions are the twelve signs of the zodiac. The signs are named after but not defined by nearby constellations. They are specific sections of ecliptic longitude.

Here's a visual of the ecliptic and the celestial equator so you can visualize what's going on with the solstices and equinoxes:

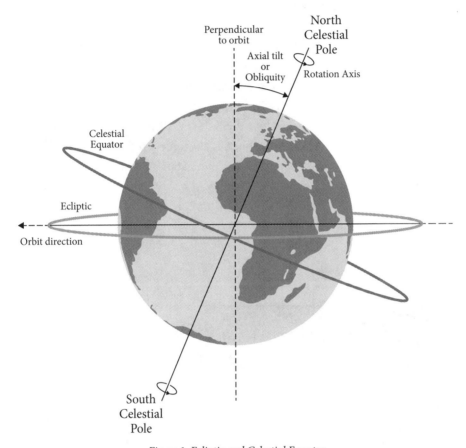

Figure 1: Ecliptic and Celestial Equator

The zodiacal (ecliptic) circle is quartered by the solstices (north–south) and equinoxes (east–west). You probably know that the equinoxes are times of equal day and night, but to fully understand them, you must know that the equinoxes (and the solstices) mark specific points in the ever-moving relationship between Sun and Earth. We are constantly in motion around the Sun and around the axis of the planet.

The equinoxes happen when the celestial equator (the circle of the equator extended out in to space) intersects the ecliptic—an event that happens twice a year. The Spring Equinox occurs as Sun is moving northward in the sky, around March 21, and the Autumn Equinox is when it is moving toward the south again, around September 21. In the zodiacal celestial coordinate system, the March equinox point is called 0 degrees of Aries, and the September equinox point is called 0 degrees of Libra.

The solstices mark the furthest point north or south of the celestial equator that the Sun travels. Think of the ecliptic as a belt. The equator marks the middle, but the belt extends 23.4 degrees of latitude above and below the equator. These furthest points of the Sun's reach are called the Tropic of Cancer and the Tropic of Capricorn. So you won't be surprised to find that at the Winter Solstice in December, when the Sun is positioned over the Tropic of Capricorn in the Southern Hemisphere, it also enters 0 degrees of the zodiacal sign of Capricorn. And, of course, the Sun's Station at the Tropic of Cancer in the Northern Hemisphere marks its entry into the zodiacal sign of Cancer.

Here are two illustrations of Earth at an equinox and solstice that illustrate what's going on:

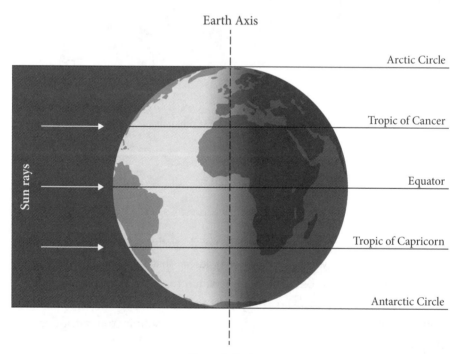

Figure 2: Equinox

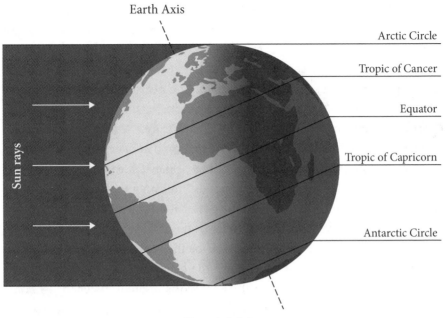

Figure 3: Solstice

What It All Means

Aries, Libra, Cancer, and Capricorn are the four cardinal signs of the zodiac,[1] and Sun (or, indeed, any of the planets) at the zero-degree mark of any of these signs is considered to be especially powerful in a horoscope. This entry into cardinal signs is what happens astrologically at the solstices and equinoxes. Both solstices and equinoxes are times of shift and change. The solstices mark a shift back from the farthest point of the Sun's travel, the equinoxes mark the fleeting moment of balance which must then immediately tip in the direction of the next solstice. Cardinal signs are known for their ability to begin things, to innovate and manifest. Their lesson is that we must establish ourselves and our dreams in the world. As Goethe said, "Whatever you can do, or dream you can do, begin it." (Goethe had Mars—the "doing" planet—in Capricorn.)

---

1. Cardinal, fixed, and mutable are the three "modes" of the zodiacal circle. Each mode is associated with four different signs, which form a cross on the zodiac. Each of those signs is ruled by a particular element—Air, Fire, Water, or Earth.

When Sun reaches the midpoint between solstice and equinox, or equinox and solstice, it will always be at 15 degrees of one of the fixed signs of the zodiac—Taurus, Leo, Scorpio, and Aquarius. Since the solstices and equinoxes quarter the zodiacal circle, these four Stations are known as the cross-quarters because they further divide the quartered ecliptic. The signs the cross-quarters fall in offer the purest, most stable expression of their respective element—Taurus is Earth, Leo is Fire, Scorpio is Water, and Aquarius is Air. The lesson of the fixed signs is that we can live fully in the moment, while still recognizing that change is inevitable.

Some people see the quarter Sabbats as indicating the beginning of their respective seasons. Others prefer to mark beginnings with the cross-quarters. For example, some consider Samhain, the Scorpio midpoint between Autumn Equinox and Winter Solstice, to be the beginning of winter, and the beginning of a New Year. Others mark the beginning of the Year at Winter Solstice, with Samhain marking the apotheosis of autumn's energies. Some begin the new year at the Spring Equinox. Personally, I keep in mind that this is the circle of the seasons—there is no beginning, and there is no end. There is only change. I celebrate the beginning of winter at Samhain, and the beginning of the new year at Winter Solstice.

These eight points, eight Stations of the Sun, are powerful locations in the zodiac. Planets at these points are strengthened in a horoscope by that placement. The four cardinal points, considered as a whole, are known as the Aries Point, and they tend to indicate public exposure (even if your "public" is just your local community), and/or events that initiate changes.

The four fixed points offer the power of certainty and stability, the full strength of that sign's element. Visionary astrologer Dane Rudhyar called these four points "the gates of the avatar," suggesting an opening in the Veil between the physical realm and the world of spirit. Indeed, Samhain and Beltane, two Sabbats that are traditionally known for opening the veil between the worlds of flesh and spirit, fall on the Scorpio and Taurus midpoints, respectively.

So now we have eight Stations of the Sun, approximately six weeks apart, each with both astrological and astronomical significance. No matter what your personal beliefs are about spirituality and religion, if you are looking for a perfectly natural way to celebrate the seasons and the Web of Life, this is a good framework to start with. You can create celebrations around each Station, working with your preferred spiritual/archetypal/symbolic elements, and use them as a time to review your own life, looking at where you've been and where you're going.

I'll retain the Wiccan names throughout the book because they are meaningful—they're symbols in their own right. But I encourage you to make up your own names if the Wiccan ones don't suit you (I'll offer some alternates, too). The sections on the Stations will help you develop holiday celebrations that are tailored to your beliefs and the ecosystem in which you live.

You can adapt these celebrations to your environment and the accompanying seasonal changes. What's blooming or not at this time of year? From which direction do the storms usually come? Is there rain, or is it a drought season? How do the seasons' weather patterns make you feel?

If you are in the southern hemisphere, you will probably want to flip the Sabbats to fit your seasons. For instance, your Winter Solstice celebration would happen in June. But since I am in the Northern Hemisphere, I am not going to try to tell those of you down under how to switch things around because I have no clue. I have, however, included several books that will help you in the resources section. So I'll be describing the Stations from a northern perspective.

But no matter where you are on Earth, the astrology stays the same—e.g., the Sun enters the sign of Cancer in June in both hemispheres. Also, the days of these Stations vary by one or two days every year. Check with an ephemeris, or your friendly neighborhood astrologer or astronomer for the exact date. Or stop by my Facebook page—www.facebook.com/uraniaswell/—and leave a message if you have any questions!

Resources

Ronald Hutton, *The Stations of the Sun: A History of the Ritual Year in Britain* (Oxford: Oxford University Press, 2001).

Mike Nichols, *The Witches' Sabbats* (Portland: Acorn Guild Press, 2005).

Pauline Campanelli and Dan Campanelli, *Wheel of the Year: Crafting a Magical Life* (St. Paul: Llewellyn Publications, 1988).

Patricia Monaghan, *Seasons of the Witch* (Oak Park: Delphi Press, 1992).

H. Byron Ballard, *Earth Works: Ceremonies in Tower Time* (Asheville: Smith Bridge Press, 2018).

Frances Billinghurst, *Dancing the Sacred Wheel: A Journey through the Southern Sabbats* (South Downs: TDM Publishing, 2012).

Raven Grimassi, *Crafting Wiccan Traditions: Creating a Foundation for Your Spiritual Beliefs & Practices* (St. Paul: Llewellyn Publications, 2008).

Jane Meredith, *Rituals of Celebration: Honoring the Seasons of Life through the Wheel of the Year* (St. Paul: Llewellyn Publications, 2013).

Tiffany Lazic, *The Great Work: Self-Knowledge and Healing Through the Wheel of the Year* (St. Paul: Llewellyn Publications, 2015).

CHAPTER TWO
Science on the Bleeding Edge

M any people simply avoid thinking much about magic and spirituality because they believe it is illogical and "anti-science" to even consider the existence of nonphysical beings or any kind of intelligent awareness or communication that is not focused in a physical body. Certainly many (but not all) scientists believe this.

This chapter on the current state of science as it relates to magic and spirituality is necessarily brief. It would take an entire book (several of which have, fortunately, been written and are noted at the end) to explain, in depth and detail, the current scientific paradigms and breakthroughs regarding what scientists refer to as parapsychology, or psi, and the role of consciousness in creating reality. But I spent many years trying to integrate my scientific education with my metaphysical interests and experiences, so I want to point out some specific thoughts and ideas for your consideration that were helpful to me in that process. You'll note that I am not interpreting the discoveries of quantum mechanics myself but building on the clearly articulated interpretations of highly qualified, even revered, physicists.

The mainstream scientific consensus is that reality is entirely physical, that there is no reality beyond what we can perceive with our five senses. In which case, anything we perceive as "spirit" or "nonphysical consciousness" is simply imaginary—the result of random chemical reactions in the brain, which has apparently not evolved beyond this drastic misperception of reality. In this view, consciousness is created within the physical brain as a result of physical processes. There is no such thing as a soul, and our existence ends with the death of our bodies. Religion and spirituality are no more than codified ideas about how we should live combined with "fantasies" of powerful nonphysical beings who can affect the physical world and "delusions" of magic, miracles, and an afterlife.

But as science draws ever closer to understanding the very foundations of reality, things have gotten very, very weird, and now there are more than a few respected, highly qualified physicists and other scientists who are considering the possibility of consciousness as the ground state of reality. This is a shocking idea because they can't even agree on a definition for "consciousness." If you think about it, the concept of Consciousness as the Source, the ground of being, is on a par with the foundational belief of most religions. After all, what is God, or whatever you call the ultimate creator, if not a conscious being who exists independent of time, space, and physical reality? You can't bring something into existence if you don't exist first. Even religions that do not posit a creator in the same way the Abrahamic religions do still believe in some form of creative higher mind or awareness toward which we can strive.

Many, if not most, physicists admit that consciousness appears to be necessary to the process of creation at a quantum level but consider its role to be simply that of an observer, with no creative agency, or even as just a black box or a placeholder for something else, as yet undiscovered. But others see it as something much more foundational. In their book *You Are the Universe*, physicist Menas Kafatos, Ph.D., and Deepak Chopra, M.D., write: "Each living entity creates its own perceptual reality by interacting with the fundamental ground of existence, pure consciousness. Pure consciousness is a field of all possibilities... The womb of creation is beyond space, time, matter, and energy."[2]

When asked "Do you think that consciousness can be explained in terms of matter and its laws?" in an interview, Nobel prize–winning physicist Max Planck, one of the originators of quantum theory, responded with: "No. I regard consciousness as fundamental. I regard matter as derivative from

2. Menas C. Kafatos and Deepak Chopra, *You Are the Universe: Discovering Your Cosmic Self and Why It Matters* (New York: Harmony Books, 2017), 251.

consciousness. We cannot get behind consciousness. Everything that we talk about, everything that we regard as existing, postulates consciousness."[3]

Physicist Richard Conn Henry, academy professor of physics and astronomy at Johns Hopkins University says: "The illusion of matter, which is to say the illusion of a really existing world, is so strong, that I think most scientists are unable to overcome it. It took me decades to finally realize that this is not a joke, and that the universe is purely mental: that mind is fundamental; matter merely an illusion—and that this is physics, not philosophy (or religion)."[4]

In this more expansive view of reality, the brain is more like a radio receiver that translates consciousness into physical reality, and Consciousness is the ultimate creator. This view postulates Consciousness as the source and background reality of our physical experience. Consciousness both creates and fully inhabits physical reality. There is nothing that is not Consciousness.

You may have noted by now that I capitalize Consciousness. I do this when referring to the ultimate field of awareness that creates reality. If you want to think of Consciousness as God or Goddess, or Tao, Brahman, or All That Is, you go right ahead. The name isn't what's important. Also, "grit your teeth, clutch your crystals, and wish really hard to create a brand-new red Mercedes in your driveway!" is *not* the kind of reality creation we're talking about here. This kind of all-too-common over-simplification has no place in any serious metaphysical discussion.

Once your viewpoint encompasses Consciousness as the creative force behind the existence of all we perceive, then our spiritual explorations can be seen as human attempts to expand personal consciousness into a greater awareness of Consciousness. Our lives are not lived in a clockwork universe, but in an infinitely creative one. And we are—all of us—co-creators in this journey into a physical world.

If you take a broad and sweeping view of science, you could say that its overarching goals are to come to a deeper understanding of the reality of the human experience, how it is created, and how we can change it. Religion

---

3. The Observer, 25 January, 1931, p.17, "Interviews With Great Scientists. VI.—Max Planck." Interview by J. W. N. Sullivan.

4. Prof. Richard Conn Henry, "Review of *The God Theory* by Bernard Haish" for the *Journal of Scientific Exploration,* date unknown. http://henry.pha.jhu.edu/haisch.html (accessed January 30, 2019).

could make the same claims. But all too often these goals get overlooked, and both science and religion find themselves defending dogma rather than searching for answers.

To understand why the authorities of modern science are so often in conflict with those who profess the existence of any spiritual reality, from the doctrines of organized religion to the vaguest of New Age hand waving, we must understand two things about science and scientists. First, science has always been firmly based in the concept of a shared, measurable, objective reality. This concept has served us well through centuries of Newtonian physics, leading to an unparalleled understanding of the underlying structure of our world. But quantum mechanics can be interpreted to indicate that pure objectivity is an illusion, albeit a persistent one. If Consciousness is the source of reality rather than a byproduct of the brain, then all bets are off, and we are looking at the advent of an earth-shaking scientific revolution.

Even independent verification fails as an experimental protocol if it is discovered that we are able to connect with (or are constantly connected to) each other on a subconscious telepathic level, and there is plenty of solid research that concludes that telepathy does exist. Even if the experiments show only a very weak effect, it rips the blindfold off of double-blind experiments. And if objectivity and independent verification come into question (and they have), then while it does not negate the tremendous strides science has made, it does mean that the entire underlying structure of science needs to be overhauled.

It's kind of like finding out that the foundation of your large, expensive house is badly cracked and falling apart. You know this is going to be a big deal and your life is going to change dramatically. You may alter the house in other ways while you are fixing the foundation and end up with a way better house than you started out with. But it's still going to be a major disruption in your life—expensive, time-consuming, emotionally draining, mentally exhausting. Scientific revolutions entail a lot of foundation fixing. Anyone whose career (not to mention deeply-held beliefs) is built on the foundation of materialism would have a difficult time of it if it is shown that the universe is, as Dr. Henry suggested, "purely mental: that mind is fundamental; matter merely an illusion—and that this is physics, not philosophy (or religion)."[5] No wonder so many of them are so resistant to the idea of a spiritual reality. Revolution is never easy.

Second, scientists are human and subject to all the usual human faults and failings. Though they like to see themselves as pioneers of rational, objective thinking, going where the evidence takes them, they are just as influenced by subconscious forces, repressed emotions, and primal survival concerns as the rest of us. Most have at least a touch of the control freak about them too (it goes with the territory—the whole "discovering the secrets of the universe" thing). Yes, they learn specific, rational ways of looking at and analyzing a problem via the scientific method. They are taught to think as objectively as possible, and even to write in the passive voice, in order to distance themselves from their data.

But they are not trained—at least, not in any standard scientific curriculum —to cultivate the observer within themselves, to grapple with their fears, their emotional blocks, and personal delusions that are fed by unfaced and unintegrated childhood traumas. Those who think their work is unaffected by these considerations are deluding themselves. Those who admit to their psychological issues, explore their own minds, and develop their inner observer, are much better able to be objective and impartial in their scientific work.

Many magical groups insist that their members undergo some form of psychological counseling before and often during their magical training. This would, no doubt, be helpful to scientists as well because anyone who has undertaken psychological self-analysis learns that when a particular event or topic elicits overwhelmingly strong emotions, there are almost always unconscious forces driving our reactions and behavior. (Unconscious forces are mental/emotional processes, often set in place in childhood, that are inaccessible to conscious awareness but influence judgments, feelings, or behavior.) This is understandable, but not objective at all, and if one has not developed the skills needed to uncover and work with the unconscious, then they will be unaware of the bias they bring to their scientific opinions.

---

5. Henry, "Review of *The God Theory* by Bernard Haish."

Whenever I find scientists frothing at the mouth over a topic such as astrology or reincarnation, I suspect the over-reaction is due to an unconscious fear that these ideas, if proven, threaten the very basis of the science in which they have invested so much of their time and effort. It would put their entire lives in upheaval. When looked at closely, the evidence they cite to back up their assertions of "pseudoscience" frequently doesn't stand up to any reasonable scrutiny, and the emotional reactions suggest that the rational mind has been locked in its room, leaving more primal concerns in charge. Sometimes, they won't even look at the valid, peer-reviewed research that supports the ideas they reject.

As you may have already figured out, the view of Consciousness as the source and ground of reality is the approach that fits with my own experiences and the experiences of mystics through the centuries and across cultures. It is strongly resisted by the clockwork scientists, who are convinced that life is the result of chance combinations of chemicals and various physical forces. They will not listen to any talk of psychic abilities, enlightenment, reincarnation, spirits, or the creative power of Consciousness. They say that Consciousness is simply a placeholder in their equations. At most, it's an observer, not a creator. Yes, it's a bit of a black box, but they'll figure it out; and when they do it will be entirely physical and mathematical. They are quite certain of that!

But while quantum mechanics has led to some remarkable applications in the real world (almost all of our information technology, for instance, is based on principles of quantum mechanics), there are still large gaps in the theories, and rather a lot of hand waving going on to explain those gaps. It's kind of hard to have to deal with something in your equations that you can't even define—and we don't have a good definition of consciousness, much less Consciousness. There are multiple "interpretations" of quantum mechanics, meaning theories about how the mathematics correspond with reality. An interpretation that sees Consciousness being the ultimate cause (a.k.a. the "consciousness causes collapse" interpretation) is one of about fifteen or so current interpretations, and while it is certainly controversial, it is held by a number of respected physicists.

Back in 1962, M.I.T. physicist, scientific historian, and philosopher Thomas S. Kuhn published a book called *The Structure of Scientific Revolu-*

tions, which is still considered a landmark in the field. Kuhn proposed that scientific progress is not linear but marked by periods of revolutionary ideas interspersed with periods of which he referred to as "normal science." The work done by scientists during these "normal" periods solidifies and clarifies the ideas of the previous revolutions.

Normal science, Kuhn suggested, operates under a certain paradigm, an overarching model or standard that is, eventually, challenged so deeply by new discoveries that the entire paradigm must change to encompass them. These discoveries lead first to crisis, then to a revolution that unseats the old paradigm and puts a new one in its place. I believe we are at one of those crisis points now, and it is centered around the role of Consciousness in the creation of the reality we experience.

We need a new vocabulary. We need a vision. We need to be able to talk about our experiences if we are going to explore them. The idea that spirituality and science must be kept separate is self-defeating. Both science and spirituality seek to discover truth, and both have much to contribute to the exploration. There are not two truths. If spiritual experiences are real, then they are real in the scientific sense and can ultimately be made sense of—though perhaps not fully understood—from a scientific perspective. Otherwise, those experiences are no more than flights of imagination with no grounding in reality.

Scientists and priests do not—cannot—have all the answers to the mysteries of life on Earth. Those of us layfolk who sense something more, who tune in to a larger reality, who travel far enough on the spectrum of consciousness to see beyond the deeply challenging and problematic reality we have created here to the possibilities of peace, joy, and ecstatic creation, can help point the way to a deeper scientific understanding of reality. We may not have the math, but math is the map here, not the territory.

My core assumption in this book is that Consciousness creates reality, not the other way around. We don't have consciousness because we have a brain, we have a brain because we are Consciousness and partake of its creative powers. Consciousness is not separate from us in any way. It is in every atom and particle in our universe and also fully transcendent. It exists whether or not our physical universe does. Our universe exists because it is Consciousness. This concept has been postulated by both mystics and an increasing number of scientists—though mystics have been at it for a lot longer. I'll discuss the hows and whys of this in subsequent chapters, but for now, let's just take that as a given.

I've done a fair amount of reading and taken a couple of courses on quantum physics for the non-physicist, so I'm reasonably well-educated in the topic for a lay person. It's a fascinating study, particularly when combined with an in-depth study of mysticism and mystical traditions. I recommend it if your curiosity leads you in that direction. I've included several excellent texts written for lay people by theoretical physicists and other scientists from other disciplines in the resources if you want to learn more.

But the point I want to make here is that you can pursue your spiritual studies without necessarily being "unscientific." The world of spirit that mystics and shamans speak of is open to us all. The spirit world is simply another expression of Consciousness, one that interfaces with the physical world. If the world of spirit is real, then it is something we all share and it is way bigger than we are. At some point, Consciousness becomes time and space, becomes physical, and at some point, scientists will likely discover how that happens. They seem to be getting close now.

But that doesn't mean we can't explore that world using the signal receiver of our brain and the guidance of mystics who have walked these roads before us. We may not have the math to describe it, but we have words, and we have experiences, and we have the changes that happen in our lives when we consciously work with spirit, with Consciousness. And we have lots of anecdotal evidence that can help us develop our ideas.

Anecdotal evidence, though often spoken of with scorn, is, in fact, integral to science. Because it's the anecdotal evidence that gets us wondering, that points the way to the question that sparks the hypothesis that leads to the experiment that gives us solid experimental data and a working theory. As long as we recognize the limits of anecdotal evidence, we can certainly use it to explore and assess our spiritual views and practices, particularly because (and this is something many people seem to forget) scientific experimentation takes a lot of expertise, time, and money.

Finding scientists and funds to look into topics such as psi, reincarnation, remote viewing, telepathy, and spirit contact is exceptionally difficult because these scientists can usually add "ruining my career" to the time and funding problems that normally plague research. The prejudice against these subjects is so strong that once a scientist has become associated with this kind of work, they are almost certainly going to be blackballed by mainstream scientists.

The perceived split between science and spirituality is manufactured. Humans have been perceiving and interacting with a world outside of the physical reality to which we are primarily attuned for millennia. It's possible that all these experiences are the result of chance chaos in the brain, or misperception of reality due to evolutionary dead-ends. It's also possible—even likely—that reality is far larger than we have ever imagined before, that time and space are indeed illusions, and we have an existence that transcends our bodies, space, and time.

What does your own experience tell you? If you aren't sure of the answer to this question, then following up on some of the ideas, tools, and techniques in this book will give you the opportunity to see for yourself that it is possible to expand and deepen your awareness of your Greater Self, to become a more complex, aware, and influential person, to create your own life in your own unique way, in unique relationships with others.

Most practitioners of various religions and spiritual disciplines insist that the world of spirit *is* real—magic, meditation, and prayer produce real-world changes; the subtle body and subtle energies can be manipulated through both physical and mental means; gods and other beings of spirit actually exist; telepathy and other psychic abilities exist and can be developed; we have a soul that survives death. So it surprises me when some of these very same people reject any connection between science and spirituality and insist that science cannot understand or define the world of spirit, nor should it even try. Because to say this is to say the world of spirit is, in fact, not real but a figment of our imaginations. If it's real, it comes under the purview of science, and our understanding of reality will continue to expand. But, as always, intuition and experiential awareness will precede any illumination of reason.

Is there a world of spirit that both fully inhabits and transcends our time-and-space physical realm? I believe that there is, and I've been exploring it for decades. If you can consider that Consciousness is Source and are willing to expand your perceptions of the world, then you might enjoy exploring it too. One of the best ways I've found to do this is by developing a magical practice. Magic is the science of the inner world and the otherworld. It is generated internally and reflected in the outer world. But magic is a word mired in misperceptions, so in the next chapter we'll take a look at what magic really is.

Resources

Amit Goswami, Ph.D., *The Self-Aware Universe: How Consciousness Creates the Material World* (New York: TarcherPerigee, 1995).

Bruce Rosenblum and Fred Kuttner, *Quantum Enigma: Physics Encounters Consciousness* (Oxford: Oxford University Press, 2011).

Dean Radin, Ph.D., *The Conscious Universe: The Scientific Truth of Psychic Phenomena* (New York: HarperOne, 1997).

Robert McLuhan, *Randi's Prize: What Sceptics Say about the Paranormal, Why They Are Wrong, and Why It Matters* (Leicester: Troubadour Publishing, 2010).

Edward F. Kelly and Adam Crabtree, *Beyond Physicalism: Toward Reconciliation of Science and Spirituality* (Lanham: Rowman & Littlefield, 2015).

Menas C. Kafatos and Deepak Chopra, *You Are the Universe: Discovering Your Cosmic Self and Why It Matters* (New York: Harmony Books, 2017).

Thomas Kuhn, *The Structure of Scientific Revolutions* (Chicago: University of Chicago Press; 3rd edition, 1996).

Stephen S. Carey, *A Beginner's Guide to Scientific Method* (Boston: Cengage Learning; 4th edition, 2011).

Online

Institute of Noetic Sciences, http://www.noetic.org.

"Why Magical Thinking Isn't Crazy," a course taught by physicist York Dobbins, Ph.D., through Cherry Hill Seminary, http://www.cherryhillseminary.org.

Oliver Burkeman, "Why can't the world's greatest minds solve the mystery of consciousness?" accessed January 15, 2019, https://www.theguardian.com/science/2015/jan/21/-sp-why-cant-worlds-greatest-minds-solve-mystery-consciousness.

Richard Conn Henry, "The Mental Universe," accessed January 15, 2019, http://henry.pha.jhu.edu/mentaluniverse.pdf.

Dean Radin, Ph.D., "New Experiments Show Consciousness Affects Matter," accessed January 15, 2019, https://youtu.be/nRSBaq3vAeY.

CHAPTER THREE
Magic(k)

The kind of magic I'll be discussing here involves diving down the rabbit hole of expanded reality, not pulling the poor things out of hats by their ears. This magic involves practice and discipline and contemplation, not sleight of hand. (The spelling "magick" is used frequently in some magical traditions to differentiate the spiritual practice from stage magic. I'll use the usual spelling of "magic" in this book, but now you know what the alternative spelling means when you see it.)

The most common definitions of magic by practitioners of the art in the West are usually some variation on Aleister Crowley's "Magick is the Science and Art of causing Change to occur in conformity with Will."[6] I find Crowley's definition to be a bit broad. If I want to watch a different TV channel and I pick up the remote and change it, I'm causing change to occur in conformity with my will. But it's not magic. I would say that magic is influencing reality in accordance with one's will through direct, conscious, trained use of the mind and emotions.

People usually turn to magic because they want to change their lives. Those who choose to seriously study and practice it discover that it changes their consciousness first and then it changes their lives. If Consciousness is the creative force behind the manifest universe, and we are part of that Consciousness, then we, too, are a creative force—whether we practice magic or not. But when we become aware of our creative abilities and deliberately work to improve them, then we become magicians.

---

6. Aleister Crowley, *Magick: Liber Aba*, York Beach, ME: Red Wheel/Weiser, 1994.

Working with our minds this way does not involve rote repetition of affirmations while clutching a wand and ruthlessly repressing the unintegrated fears of our unconscious, our shadow. The practice of magic involves mental discipline, emotional courage, and deep work to release past programming (in this life and others) that has left so many of us swimming in a toxic emotional stew of shame and fear. Our culture is unhealthy, and our culture has its own powerful magic.

But we also affect our culture, and we can make a difference. It's the work of a lifetime to heal ourselves, share the healing, and creatively manifest our dreams in the world. But it starts, always, with learning to harness our thoughts and emotions in service to our personal, soul-level vision. Then, having trained our minds, explored our emotions, and integrated the power inherent in the shadow, we have a much stronger psychic effect on the zeitgeist because this work widens our circle of influence.

Many magicians, myself included, are animists, which means we believe everything—every atom and photon—partakes of Consciousness, is connected through Consciousness, and so contributes to our co-creation of the reality we experience here within the boundaries of time and space. Magicians talk a lot about intention, and our individual intention is where magic begins. But reality is a joint creation, and so magic must be too. Successful magic is never a solo endeavor, even if there is only one human doing the magical work. Creating with magic involves opening to shared consciousness, weaving strands of energy from Nature and spirit to create what we envision, strengthen our influence, and expand our awareness.

If we are, in fact, direct participants in the creation of physical reality, then we have clearly created a world in which we influence and are influenced—by each other, by Nature, and by spiritual realities of which we may be unaware, such as influences from past lives, ancestors, guides, and even spiritual parasites. As we train our minds, our inner eyes, to inhabit a larger reality, we see the energies surrounding us more clearly and can make more informed choices about which ones we invite into our creation.

Symbols

A big part of magical work involves a conscious focus on symbols, so understanding exactly what symbols are and what they do is important to an understanding of magic. Symbols are not just a visible shorthand for something else or a mathematical sign or an icon on your computer, though they can be all those things. The symbols we work with in magic, though, have an emotional and spiritual component. They are packed with power and a level of understanding that is directly communicated to us on all levels: physical, mental, emotional, and spiritual. Our reasoning mind can play with them, but they contain way more information than our reasoning minds can process.

We have elevated our reasoning human mind to what we perceive as the pinnacle of our civilization. We credit it with bringing us out of the ancestral caves of the hunter-gatherer, with allowing us considerable control over our environment and comforts unimaginable to those ancestors. But our reasoning mind is like an adolescent athlete glorying in the strength of her newly matured body, certain that she can conquer the world. She feels invincible. She has not yet understood that true mastery of any athletic skill is attained only through experience and consistent discipline. She thinks she knows it all, but she doesn't know the half of it.

Our cultural attitude toward the reasoning human mind is not dissimilar. We think we know it all, or we are very close to knowing it all, but that simply isn't the case. Consider this: the universe exists in its fullness whether we can reason it out or not. If you were to hop in a Tardis and travel back to chat with one of your hunter-gatherer ancestors, you would be frustrated if you were to try to explain modern life to them. They could not understand calculus, for instance, because they wouldn't have had basic math. But what we now call the principles of calculus existed back then, they just hadn't been discovered—which might make you curious about what else is still undiscovered, at least by our reasoning minds.

If Consciousness is Source, then the universe has information for us that our reasoning minds are simply not yet ready to comprehend. Remember, we are part of that Consciousness. We have access to the whole shebang; it's just a question of how much we can encompass through reason from our perspective as an individual within time and space. How much we can comprehend of the vastness around us, the infinity? In fact, we'll never understand it all. There will always be more to discover, more to the Great Mystery, and symbols are often the key to those discoveries, clues that lead us on to solve some of our own smaller mysteries.

If you've ever taken a chemistry class, then you've most likely heard of the benzene ring because its discovery was a major breakthrough in the understanding of molecular structure. It was discovered by Friedrich August Kekulé, who was puzzling over the problem when he dozed off and dreamed of the ouroboros—a snake swallowing its own tail. This gave him the idea of the ring structure for the molecule. It was the symbol, sourced from his unconscious, that helped him make the intellectual breakthrough. Dreams are almost always symbolic and are the source of a surprising number of scientific breakthroughs. Our unconscious is tuned in to the larger forces of the universe, and it speaks to us in symbols.

Symbols work through all our levels of awareness—conscious, subconscious, and unconscious. Those words mean different things to different people, so I'll define my terms here before we go on, since my definitions don't entirely conform to standard psychological definitions. I also don't believe there are hard-line demarcations between these three levels of consciousness; they are interconnected and make up the whole of who we are.

When we are conscious, we are focused in physical reality, aware of our surroundings, able to reason, interact with others, and take deliberate actions. This is our normal waking state. To use a computer metaphor, the conscious state is what's currently in the computer's RAM, its memory, what we are working on now.

The subconscious is like the computer's hard drive. There's a lot of personal information stored on there, along with a lot of "programs"—personal and cultural structures of belief, knowledge, and memory that we are tied into and use in our daily lives.

The unconscious is like the internet—it connects us to our Greater Self, to the collective, and many other sources of information.

Increasing self-awareness and the use of symbols allows us to navigate all these levels and become more conscious of who we are, the information we have available to us, and our place in the universe.

The conscious mind is our reasoning mind, and it has its own language—the language we use on a daily basis. But that language cannot take our mind beyond the boundaries of the software we are using to navigate through life—our current level of awareness, the extent of our knowledge. There's more to reality, and to Consciousness, but we can't access that knowledge using the software of our reasoning mind. We need to expand beyond our spread-sheets and word processors that say "File" and "Open" and "Print" in English or Spanish or Japanese or whatever our daily language is. We need to learn to communicate with the operating system that lives in our subconscious and then connect to the internet of our unconscious if we want to expand beyond what we can grasp with our reasoning minds. We need to learn code, and symbols are the code that connects us to our soul, to that part of our-selves that is not confined to time and space. Symbols connect us to the universe, and to a greater awareness of Consciousness.

Symbols have an emotional component, which can be quite powerful. Witness people's devotion or highly negative reactions to a flag of a country or particular group (the Confederate flag is an excellent example of this) or a simple geometric design (such as a cross or swastika). Sometimes symbols just ring conditioned bells of awareness, like a red octagon with the letters *S*, *T*, *O*, and *P* blazoned across it. We don't even read it—we react immediately from a subconscious place that knows and puts into practice the appropriate reactions before we are even conscious of needing to take our foot off the gas and put it on the brake. We live much of our lives from this subconscious place.

We are like icebergs; there's a lot of who we are below the surface of our everyday awareness, and we are only vaguely aware of it, if at all. Yet these emotions, memories, beliefs, thoughts, awareness of past lives—all these things—drive our behavior, our responses and reactions, and our everyday existence. We can connect more consciously to them, use them as a source of energy for change, and enhance our understanding of the breadth and depth of our existence if we embrace the use of symbols and develop our own sym-bol library because the symbols help us communicate over a wide range of awareness and consciousness.

The art and science of magic—for it is both—requires that we expand our awareness and extend our consciousness so we can creatively express more of who we are and have a greater influence on our physical world. To do this, we need to be able to travel into a larger reality while not losing our grounding within time and space. Symbols come in very handy on those travels because they allow us to communicate beyond the current limits and boundaries of our reasoning mind. Symbols allow us to experience and comprehend—at least to some degree—what is far beyond our current understanding.

The Creative Universe

If Consciousness is, in fact, the ultimate source of our reality, then Consciousness is the ultimate creative force. And if all that exists is not—cannot be—separate from Consciousness, but is part and parcel of it, then as conscious beings, we are, ourselves, creators. If we have the will, ability, and freedom to create, then we are not puppets. We're not separate from and manipulated by a cosmic puppet master, nor are we simply the result of random chance. But it sure seems like we are sometimes, doesn't it? I mean, if we are creators, then how come it seems like we're just tossed into life? After all, we didn't ask to be born, right?

Or did we?

Each one of us, the essence of our being, is much larger than our everyday consciousness. If we are part of Consciousness, then our seeming separation from it and from each other is an illusion, a creative endeavor on the part of Consciousness. At some point, as our awareness increases and expands, we see beyond the limits of time and space, into the wider awareness from which our limited world is created. But most of us have not arrived at that point yet, outside of our nightly dreams and occasional flashes of insight and enlightenment. Many people probably agree with my father, who used to say, "I don't believe in God because I can't believe an all-knowing and all-powerful being would do such a piss-poor job of designing the world."

But if you consider the world from the perspective of Consciousness who is looking to create whatever can be created, then maybe, if you were Consciousness, you'd start by putting some limits on your latest project. That's what artists and creators do—they start by defining the limits of their creation. There's an edge to the canvas; the piece of marble for the statue is so big and no bigger, shaped in just this way; the book must fit between covers; and the building must fit on a specific piece of land, using available materials.

Our ultimate limits in this world are time and space. And within those limits, Consciousness placed itself and allowed itself/us to have free will, then erased from our limited consciousnesses most of the knowledge of who we really are and where we came from. Because that was a way to create something completely new—to allow us to forget that we already are Consciousness and come into the fullness of our creative natures from an almost blank slate.

The philosophy/theology can get rather intense and complex, and you'll probably want to explore these ideas further on your own. I'll discuss them more in chapter 5, and, of course, offer some books to spark your own philosophizing. My own conclusion is that the universe is ultimately creative and that each one of us is part of a Greater Self. That self is fully aware of its existence within Consciousness, the One Mind, and chose to be part of this creation—not for just one life, but for many.

I believe that the physical realm is a creative endeavor of Consciousness and that our Greater Selves, fully aware, chose to be part of this creative endeavor, knowing that we would not remember making that choice, that we would not remember the larger context of our existence, once we dove in. Diving into time and space is a full-immersion, free-will experience where we forget what we were before we came here and have the ability to create joy and beauty, pain and ugliness, whatever we can imagine within the limits of the world we are born into. We do not create alone. Our world is a collective effort with every other being on the planet (and probably other planets as well). It's part of the creative challenge we take on to establish a life for ourselves and then grow into a remembrance and deeper understanding of where we came from.

We are never truly separated from that larger reality. There is always a connection, we all have this inner well of energy, information, and emotion that connects our everyday consciousness to our Greater Self, to our soul, and to our own memories, both of this incarnation and others. There are places we go—in dreams, in meditation, in fleeting moments of awareness—to explore different levels of reality, to reconnect with the source our creative energy. We can travel to many levels in our dreams, but part of the magician's work is to be able to do it with conscious awareness in order to influence and create within physical life.

The Difference Between Magic and Snake Oil

Now let's take a closer look at this idea of magic as a way to "create your own reality," since purveyors of prosperity snake oil and other metaphysical nostrums have made it sound as though if you aren't rich/healthy/happy it's because of your lack of willpower/character/a dose of their nostrums. There is a distinct odor of self-interest and lack of empathy around the whole concept, and people are put off by it, understandably.

But reality is far more complex and nuanced than we can even imagine, and its creation certainly cannot be condensed into a nostrum. Let's look a bit deeper at this whole business of how we do or do not create, shift, or change the reality we experience.

If Consciousness is the source of the reality we experience, then clearly Consciousness chose to create a highly complex, three-dimensional reality within set boundaries of time and space, to which we all—as part of that Consciousness—contribute. We aren't standing around creating Disney-esque landscapes with a sweep of our wands. But on some deep level, the individual consciousnesses of every human (and animal and plant and atom) helps create our shared reality by weaving together in an intricate and ever-changing design. This weaving, this dance of energy, happens at a level we cannot keep in our consciousness while we are hard-wired into a body and focused within time and space. Which is not to say we can't access it, but we can't live there.

My own experiences have led me to believe that we consciously choose our parents and birth circumstances with certain lessons and experiences in mind, but we pack that awareness away at a very early age because we must in order to live our physically focused lives. But let's take the point of view of our Greater Self for a moment, and even the Greater Self of our Greater Self. Consciousness is big. Consciousness is complex, and Consciousness is, ultimately, creative. So let's return to that idea that Consciousness decided it wanted to explore the possibilities of creating within the limits of time and space, and that this creative project has resulted in us, here, with little or no memory of where we came from but having both the power to act within this realm, and what appears to be the free will to act or react as we choose. What if we are here because we, as our Greater Self, decided that we wanted to be part of this fascinating creation of Consciousness, not just for one lifetime, but for many.

What if we wanted to see what we could do within the chosen confines of time and space in the same way an artist chooses to paint within the boundaries of a canvas or carve a statue from a single piece of marble? What if things took a difficult twist and we collectively ended up creating a world in which war and pain and victimhood became commonplace? What if we could change that, and we knew it, but we had to change it from within? What if we had to rediscover our own creative capabilities as part of Consciousness?

I'm not saying that's the way it is. I'm only suggesting that you consider the ramifications of Consciousness as Source, as the ultimate creator of reality. Consider what it might mean if every atom and molecule partook of that Consciousness, and that we, ourselves, as individuals and en masse with the all powers and curiosity of Consciousness, created the rather difficult world we live in, then allowed ourselves to forget that we were part and parcel of its creation. And we did this out of curiosity, as an experiment with ourselves as the subjects, to learn how to work within the boundaries of time and space.

If that's the case, then the difficulties and pain that are so commonplace in this world become challenges we need to work through, not punishment from some god on high or the impersonal cruelty of blind chance. We need to learn to work our way back to our awareness and power from a place of forgetfulness because in doing so we create a brand-new kind of consciousness, a whole new creation that extends and expands reality for us all.

We come to Earth with some memories of our true power and some awareness of where we came from. But as we grow, we forget. Why? Because we are exploring what can be created from within an intense focus on a time-and-space-bounded reality. We have our ultimate existence in a reality that surmounts all those pain and difficulties, but we must create our way out of them from within the limits Consciousness placed around itself.

A modern metaphor is the whole concept of virtual reality, in which machines trick our senses into believing we are experiencing something we are not—a concept explored in detail in the movie *The Matrix*. What if Consciousness, confined and directed, is the true nature of our reality? What happens when we take the red pill—the one that lets us see the world as it really is—by disciplining our brains through meditation and magic, tuning them to receive a wider frequency of Consciousness, and coming to understand how we co-create our reality, weaving a tapestry of experience in concert with all conscious beings, and with Consciousness itself?

This would mean, of course, that we can learn to create our way into a better world. That's what magicians do. That's what magic is about. We study and learn and experiment with ways of influencing reality using our minds and our emotions. We don't fully understand the mechanism that makes this thing we call magic work, but our experiences tell us that it does. And the only way you'll ever know is to give it a try yourself. I've given you some of my ideas about how it all might work, but the sensible approach is first to determine *if* it works. Then you can focus on how.

Once you've decided to give magic a shot, then give it a fair shot. If you aren't doing the work, if you are constantly second-guessing and doubting yourself, your magic will not be very effective. Here's the thing—the most scientific approach to exploring magic involves letting go of both your doubts and biases as well as any wishful thinking. You don't need to abandon your rational side—you just need to let it sit on the sidelines and observe sometimes instead of loudly insisting that this magic stuff can't possibly work. Hopefully, you'll think about it and decide that you can allow yourself to explore spirituality and magic without sacrificing your belief in science. For the next step, let's take a look at the first touchstone of our spiritual year, the Winter Solstice, or Yule.

Resources

Amber K, *True Magick* (St. Paul: Llewellyn Publications, Revised, Expanded edition, 2006).

Dean Radin, Ph.D., *Real Magic: Ancient Wisdom, Modern Science, and a Guide to the Secret Power of the Universe* (New York: Random House, 2018).

Christopher Penczak, *The Casting of Spells: Creating a Magickal Life Through the Words of True Will* (Salem: Copper Cauldron Publishing, 2016).

H. Byron Ballard, *Staubs and Ditchwater: A Friendly and Useful Introduction to Hillfolks' Hoodoo* (Asheville: Smith Bridge Press, 2017).

Aidan Wachter, *Six Ways: Approaches & Entries for Practical Magic* (Albuquerque: Red Temple Press, 2018).

Jason Miller, *The Sorcerer's Secrets: Strategies in Practical Magick* (Newburyport: New Page Books, 2009).

Laura Tempest Zakroff, *Sigil Witchery: A Witch's Guide to Crafting Magick Symbols* (St. Paul: Llewellyn Publications, 2018).

Donald Michael Kraig, *Modern Magick: Twelve Lessons in the High Magickal Arts* (St. Paul: Llewellyn Publications, 1988).

John Michael Greer, *Natural Magic: Potions and Powers from the Magical Garden* (St. Paul: Llewellyn Publications, 2000).

Scott Cunningham, *Earth Power: Techniques of Natural Magic* (St. Paul: Llewellyn Publications, 1984).

CHAPTER FOUR
Yule—The
Winter Solstice

At Winter Solstice (a.k.a. Yule, Alban Arthan) the Sun appears to stand still in the sky for three days, right around December 21 (it may vary a day or so on either side). Now it is rising as far to the south as it will go before beginning to inch northward once again. The days are as short as they will ever be, and nights are long and usually cold here in the Northern Hemisphere.

Many people celebrate Winter Solstice as the start of the new year. That's always made sense to me—Sun's change of direction starts a new cycle of life. Some Pagans celebrate the New Year six weeks earlier, at Samhain, the autumn midpoint. Personally, I treat Samhain as the beginning of the end of the year and the beginning of the season of winter. The time between Samhain and solstice feels to me like an unwinding, a releasing, as we traverse the last weeks of declining light. Sun is in a sociable sign (Sagittarius) in the weeks leading up to Winter Solstice, but the partying at this time of year always seems to have an edge to it, as though we are having fun as a way of defying death.

In your celebrations this year, as you are chatting and mingling and wassailing and making small talk and wrapping presents, stay aware of the two doorways of life—birth and death. In the time between Samhain and Yule, we acknowledge death's door; but at solstice, we consciously choose life. We connect with our Greater Self and carry our ancestral DNA forward into another cycle of life.

Winter invites us to turn within, to appreciate rest and darkness, to contemplate life, death, and the reality of spirit. But as we burn through fossil fuels—"the last hours of ancient sunlight"—to power the generators that light our winters, to create reams of plastic crap destined for the landfill, most of us tend to toss that invitation out with the scraps of wrapping paper, caught up in the cultural madness that has overtaken this holy season. We lose something precious when we do that.

Myths of divine beings born into human form at the time of the Winter Solstice are numerous and stretch back at least a thousand years before Jesus' birth. Celebrations of Winter Solstice are thought to date back to Neolithic times. This time of cold and darkness emphasizes the light of the stars, brings us into the heart of the Great Mystery, and reminds us of the vastness of the universe. In that vastness, we are reminded of what we cannot know. For many of us, not knowing is scary. We can't control what we can't know, and we have this feeling that what we don't know *can* hurt us. But the fact is, we never will know it all, and one of the lessons of this season is faith in something larger than we can fully comprehend. Faith in life, faith in the return of the Sun, and faith that love and creative energy are at the heart of the Great Mystery.

The season also shows us the light within, the light of our individual awareness, and illumines the connections, the constellations we form with other individuals, with other consciousnesses, and with something greater than ourselves. The rebirth of the light is the birth of awareness, of Consciousness, into the realm of time and space. The light within is the source of our personal power in the physical realm and it is that light which remains when others have gone out. This inner light puts our fears to rest, connects us with each other, and with the Divine. The spiritual work we do at this time should be designed to feed that spark with fuel drawn from the infinite depths of the Cauldron of Creation. Oh, and that inner light is a real thing. Our cells actually produce photons of light called "biophotons." Another fascinating example of the intersection of science and metaphysics.

Now we'll get into our first round of Touch the Earth, Kiss the Sky exercises. These suggestions for things to do and things to think about are meant to help you find your own path to spirit through your experience of and attention to the world around you and to your own mind. They are only suggestions, and I hope you will read some of the resources in each section to expand and personalize your own celebrations and meditations.

In the interest of paying attention, please start this new cycle of the seasons by getting the journal and notebook that I mentioned in the introduction. You'll be using them at every Station of the Sun and hopefully during the six weeks between each one as you chart your progress toward a more magical and spiritual life.

⊣ TOUCH THE EARTH ⊢

Where's the Sun?

Get up at sunrise as often as you can as the solstice approaches and note where in the sky the Sun is rising and how it moves a little every day. Yes, it's always in the general direction of east, but it's only directly east at the equinoxes. Now, at the December solstice, it rises in the southeast. At solstice, it reaches the Tropic of Capricorn, the southernmost point of its rising, where it will appear to stand still for three days, before it begins to move north once again. Keeping an eye on the Sun's changing position in the sky relative to the seasons and your local environment is a great way to strengthen your connection to Nature in general, and the Sun in particular.

Decorate!

You don't have to celebrate Christmas to get into the spirit of the season. What is generally known as a Christmas tree can just as easily be a Winter Solstice tree. Evergreens remind us of life's strength and persistence no matter who, what, or if we worship, and the wreath is a perfect symbol for the circle of the seasons, or the womb of the Mother Goddess. If you choose to decorate your home during this season, make the decorations your own. Know what they symbolize to you. Let yourself be reminded of the blessings of the season when you look at them.

I'll discuss personal altars in chapter 7, but if you already have one, you might consider changing what is on it to reflect the seasons. At Yule, mine is all red and green and silver and glass. For me, the green symbolizes what Dylan Thomas called "the force that through the green fuse drives the flower"—Nature's irrepressible fertility and ever-renewing life. The death we see around us in winter is only temporary. Red is the color of blood, of life, but also of the ancestors. Silver and glass symbolize many things for me, among them, the cold of winter, the beautiful clarity of ice and snow and pure awareness, the fragility of life in this cold and barren season, and the nearness of death—until the Sun returns.

Consider the Earth

Consider the environmental footprint of your holiday celebrations. If you get a tree, try to get one that is from a tree farm that uses organic growing techniques. If you don't get it from a tree farm but cut it yourself in a forest, look at the tree in relationship to the forest—is it too close to other trees to grow well or is it in a place where it will be cleared anyway for some other reason? How will cutting it impact the rest of the forest? You can consider this intuitively as well as objectively. Ask the tree if it is willing to become the symbol of your holiday celebrations, to bring its beauty and scent into your home. (Just go with your intuition here. We'll discuss communicating with trees a bit further on.) If it answers in the affirmative, then treat it with the respect that the willing sacrifice of any life deserves.

When the time comes to take the tree down, pay as much attention to its disposal as you did to acquiring it. If you have a fireplace or a wood stove, you can chop it up and burn it (carefully—evergreens flare up intensely). If you have a patch of forest on your land, you can leave it where it will decompose naturally and become habitat for wildlife. City and suburban communities usually offer disposal options for trees that involve composting or turning it into mulch. In the USA, call 211 for more information on what tree recycling options are available in your community.

Please think carefully before purchasing a fake tree. It uses dwindling, polluting resources for its manufacture, and eventually ends up as more plastic crap in the landfill. If you really want one, shop the second-hand stores for it. If you have one, don't feel guilty—we all make environmentally problematic purchases. The goal is to reduce them and increase our awareness. If you already own one, make the most of it! Decorate it, enjoy it. The best way to minimize the impact of that purchase is to appreciate it and let it help you spread the spirit of the season.

Consider how you wrap any presents you give. I like to use decorative bags because they are usually saved and reused by the recipient. If I had more artistic talent, I might use brown paper grocery bags and draw on them.

Bringing It Back Home

Of course, this season always involves celebrations. Astrologically, in the weeks leading up to Winter Solstice, Sun is in the party sign of Sagittarius (all the fire signs love to party, but Sagittarius turns it into an art form). So it's not surprising that many people find themselves caught up in a social whirlwind during this time. Once the Sun enters Capricorn at the solstice, there's a natural slowdown (though many ignore that slowdown and keep going at a crazy pace). See if you can't sense that shift and adapt yourself. Bring your focus to your home base at the solstice. Give thought and energy to strengthening the frameworks and structures (physical, mental, emotional, spiritual) that support your life. Say no to a night out for a change and stay home. Reconnect with family. Light a fire or some candles. Treat yourself to a nice warm bath. Get a good night's sleep.

Experience Stillness

As Winter Solstice approaches, take time to experience stillness. You may want to sit quietly—preferably outdoors—for a little while every day and simply pay attention to your surroundings. Or wake a few minutes early and just sit quietly. This is a good time to begin a meditation practice. Training the mind is a prerequisite to expanding consciousness and sitting quietly, paying attention to what you see, hear, taste, touch, and smell is a good way to start.

Visioning

On the night before or the morning of solstice, light a small candle—a birthday candle is fine—and let yourself imagine and experience your vision for the year ahead—the best year you can imagine. Stay with this experience until the candle burns out, or, if you are using a larger candle, put it out and relight it every night until it is gone, holding a vision of your year ahead for as long as you comfortably can. You might want to write your vision in your journal, where you can refer to it again as the year unfolds.

Solstice Morning

On the morning of solstice, rise before the dawn to greet the Sun—outdoors if at all possible. As you stand in the sunlight (even if it's behind clouds) remind yourself that you are here for a reason and that your Greater Self is fully aware of all its incarnations. Your journey is yours alone, but you are always connected to your Greater Self. Affirm that you live your life on purpose as a sovereign soul who has accepted this life as a mission, not as a victim of meaningless chance. Welcome the gift of life that the returning Sun offers, and let its light awaken the light within you.

─┤ KISS THE SKY ├─

Where You've Been

As solstice approaches and the days shorten, spend some time thinking about the year that has passed. How have you let your inner light shine this year? What is blocking that light? Often, what is blocking us are limitations we create in our own minds. Identify some of the limitations that are holding you back by writing in your journal. Then, when you've identified the limitations you're ready to get rid of, write them on small slips of paper, and burn them before the solstice, as Sun is waning, with the intention to leave those limitations behind in the old year. (Burn them carefully! Have some kind of deep fireproof dish you can drop them into as they burn and keep the paper small.)

Where You Came From

Spend some time strengthening your connection to your Greater Self. We are all physical manifestations of a being that is far too expansive to be confined within the physical world. Our Greater Self's wisdom and insight can guide us *if* we are willing to listen. We are never entirely out of contact with our Greater Self, but most of us get out of the habit of listening early on.

The best way to make this connection is by simply sitting quietly with that intention in mind. You might want to speak it out loud—something like "It is my intention to come into clear communication with my Greater Self." Then sit quietly with your journal and a pen in hand. Watch your thoughts as they arise in your mind. When a thought arises that seems like it might have come from your Greater Self, write it down. If you do this regularly, eventually you'll start sensing when you are hearing from your Greater Self and when it's just your own thoughts.

You can also pose a question and then listen for whatever answers come to you. Write them down then revisit them occasionally to see if you still think the answers were from your Greater Self or your subconscious fears and desires. Make a point of asking some questions about issues in your life that will become clearer in the short run, rather than the long, so you can see how helpful (or not) the answers were. This will help you learn to distinguish between your subconscious fears or wishful thinking, eruptions from your unconscious and the voice of your Greater Self.

Where You're Going

Think about your hopes, dreams, and visions for the year ahead. What is your soul calling you to do? Bring your visions into a clear focus as we approach Winter Solstice; then, between solstice and the calendar New Year, create a plan for how to make them happen.

Question Authority

Winter Solstice heralds the Sun's entrance into the sign of Capricorn, which means it's a great time to think about all the rules and regulations you obey. Capricorn's all about rules—but whose rules? Who tells you what you can and cannot do? What you must do? Many of the rules you follow are not yours but are set by family, job, or government.

For people on a spiritual path, it's important to expand our awareness of whose rules we are following. You might want to journal about these questions. Write them down and consider your answers carefully.

1. What rules am I following that other people have set for me?
   a. Do I agree with them? Do they serve a valid purpose?
   b. If not, why am I following them? Social acceptance? Legal necessity? Family harmony?
2. What rules am I following that were set for me in childhood or as a young adult?
   a. Do I agree with them? Do they serve a valid purpose?

b. If not, why am I following them? Is it just habit? Am I still trying to please my parents? Am I afraid of what might happen if I don't follow them?

3. What rules do I set for myself that I think are good and necessary?

a. Why are they good and necessary?

b. What do I think would happen if I broke them?

You don't need to spend a lot of time and effort thinking about this. Just pose the question to yourself—many answers will come in dreams or at odd moments of the day. When they do, grab your journal and write them down.

Now, to celebrate the solstice, pick between one and three rules you can break for good. (No more than that, because you need to keep track of how you're doing in the upcoming year.) Think about it carefully, then pick rules that are outmoded, unnecessary, and keep you confined by society's expectations instead of being your true self. Rules are usually rooted in beliefs, so you will find yourself questioning them as well.

Write about that rule in your journal and keep track of when you run across it in the new year and how you respond. Does breaking that rule or even thinking about breaking it make you uncomfortable? Or are you making a big deal of breaking it and tossing it behind you? Beware of those dramatic emotional states. Sometimes they reflect a real breakthrough, but often they are covering up the uncertainty and fear you don't want to face. Pay attention to what beliefs this work brings up and notice how changing beliefs accompany changing the rules. Then spend a little time connecting with your Greater Self. Ask for their guidance and blessings in the year ahead, both in breaking old rules and establishing new ones that serve your creative and spiritual endeavors.

Light a few candles, break a few rules, and have a very merry Yule!

Resources

John Matthews, *The Winter Solstice: The Sacred Traditions of Christmas* (Wheaton: Quest Books, 1998).

Susan Pesznecker, *Yule: Rituals, Recipes & Lore for the Winter Solstice* (Edinburgh: Canongate Books, 2008).

Christian Rätsch and Claudia Müller-Ebeling, *Pagan Christmas: The Plants, Spirits, and Rituals at the Origins of Yuletide* (Rochester: Inner Traditions, 2006).

Linda Raedisch, *The Old Magic of Christmas: Yuletide Traditions for the Darkest Days of the Year* (St. Paul: Llewellyn Publications, 2013).

Brené Brown, *The Gifts of Imperfection: Let Go of Who You Think You're Supposed to Be and Embrace Who You Are* (Center City: Hazelden Publishing, 2010).

TM Srinivasan, "Biophotons as Subtle Energy Carriers," https://www.ncbi .nlm.nih.gov/pmc/articles/PMC5433113/.

CHAPTER FIVE
Self and Cosmos

Fairly early on in my practice of meditation, I was offered a classic question in many spiritual traditions as a topic for meditation: "Who am I?" I struggled with this one for years. I struggled with it while sitting on my Yoga mat, sitting at my altar, riding on the subway, walking through the park. I figured out what I was not—my body, my thoughts, my emotions, my beliefs. And having peeled away all those externals, I was still left with an unshakeable awareness of self. I still question who I am, but I can say, without question, that "I am."

Some of the religions/spiritual traditions I studied told me that sense of self was an illusion. Others spoke of the difference between ego and our essential self. Philosophers argued the definition endlessly, and those arguments all come around at some point to conscious awareness, to what scientists refer to as the "hard problem of consciousness." That thing neither they nor anyone else are able to define adequately.

Since I am neither enlightened enough nor smart enough to sort all this out definitively, I decided on an approach that works for me in my life, which boils down to the fact that we are here, interacting as individuals (I don't mean just human individuals), and there must be some reason for that. So I rejected the idea that I should give up any thoughts of having a self that was anything more than an illusion. Then, having established to my own satisfaction that "I am," the question became how to develop as an individual in harmony with my core values—love, joy, beauty, wonder, creativity—and how to grow in awareness of the larger reality I sensed. A reality in which every individual, from an atom to a human to a star, was Consciousness, and all of Consciousness was connected as one.

Back in chapter 2, we looked at the concept of a single Consciousness that is the ground of reality, the source of being. This idea is as new as modern physics, and as ancient as some of the oldest mystical writings and oral traditions on the planet.

The Hindu sacred text known as the Devi Gita explains it thusly in the voice of the Goddess:

> I am the Sun, I am the Moon, I am the Stars; I am beast, birds, Chandalas and I am the Thief, I am the cruel hunter; I am the virtuous high-souled persons and I am the female, male, and hermaphrodite. There is no doubt in this. O Mountain! Wherever there is anything, seen or heard, I always exist there, within and without. There is nothing moving or unmoving that can exist without Me.[7]

In an essay titled "The Oneness of Mind," physicist Erwin Schrödinger (yes, the same guy who came up with the famous "Schrödinger's Cat" experiment) quoted thirteenth-century Islamic-Persian mystic Aziz Nasafi:

> On the death of any living creature the spirit returns to the spiritual world, the body to the bodily world. In this, however, only the bodies are subject to change. The spiritual world is one single spirit who stands like unto a light behind the bodily world and who, when any single creature comes into being, shines through it as through a window. According to the kind and size of the window, less or more light enters the world. The light itself however remains unchanged.[8]

---

7. Veda Vyasa and Swami Vijnanananda (trans.), *The Devî Gita: Song of the Goddess* (n.p., 2011), 17.

8. Erwin Schrodinger, *What Is Life? With Mind and Matter and Autobiographical Sketches* (Cambridge: Cambridge University Press, 2012), 128.

In the same essay, Schrödinger himself said that "multiplicity is only apparent; in truth there is only one mind."

In the Tao Te Ching, one of the foundational texts of Taoism, we learn in chapter 1 that:

> The Tao that can be told is not the eternal Tao.
> The name that can be named is not the eternal name.
> The nameless is the beginning of heaven and earth.
> The named is the mother of ten thousand things.

In chapter 42 of the text we learn that:

> The Tao begot one.
> One begot two.
> Two begot three.
> And three begot the ten thousand things.

In Vedic mythology, we have the cosmic egg, which cracked in two to form heaven and earth. Greek mythology also offers us a cosmic egg from which all things were born in the form of the god Phanes/Protogonus, as does the mythology of the Dogon tribe of West Africa.

These are all mythological takes on a concept of the creation of the universe that says the origin of the physical realm can be traced back to the original split of the One Mind, of Consciousness, into Self and Other.

So let's discuss the concept of developing our individuality, of expressing self within the world, and how we relate with others. As the light increases, we focus on our relationship with the outer world, and strong relationships require strong individuals.

Most of the world's great religions and philosophies have some concept of the Absolute, the idea that there is an ultimate reality or Consciousness that encompasses the concept of All That Is. Even materialist scientist Neil deGrasse Tyson said, "We are all connected; To each other, biologically. To the earth, chemically. To the rest of the universe atomically."[9]

---

9. Neil deGrasse Tyson, *Death by Black Hole: And Other Cosmic Quandaries* (New York: W.W. Norton, 2007).

If we assume the Absolute, the singular Consciousness that formed the reality we know, that makes up the stuff of our world while existing beyond it, then the creation of this reality would require, to begin, that this singular Consciousness separate into Self and Other. At some point, Consciousness became the multiple individual consciousnesses of our reality, and I view that initial split of Consciousness into Self and Other as the first step in manifestation within time and space. Though I work with individual goddesses and gods (you didn't think humans were the most advanced consciousnesses in the universe, did you?), I see the concept of Goddess and God as the primary two emanations of Consciousness whose interaction sparks the creation of material reality. This is Wiccan symbolism and mythology, which puts a human form on an event beyond our rational minds to give us some symbolism for understanding it. But you don't need Goddess and God or even human forms. You could see it as yin and yang, Self and Other, or the Vedic concept of the cosmic egg.

While we can never fully understand the creation of material reality, of time and space, if we accept that it originated in a singular Consciousness, then it required that the One Mind, Consciousness, first create the Other, the original illusion of separation. And if you view our reality as a creative endeavor instead of a place of suffering and sin, then this split is a sacred event, one we should honor by living a life that reveres the entire universe, the creation, and our individual selves, for we all sprang from that primary event.

Creation of a new human—not to mention most other species—is accomplished by the combining of DNA from two different parents. This is how evolution happens. Each child is unique—though we share so much, we are all different because that particular combination of DNA and external factors will not be repeated. Even in the case of identical twins, epigenetic factors (external factors that affect genetic expression), not to mention individual souls, create two unique people.

Have you ever thought about the ramifications of that uniqueness? If you believe that some kind of consciousness created this universe, then it would be useful to ask, "What does this creator/consciousness really value? Judging by what we can see of the creation, what is of particular importance to the Creator, to Consciousness?"

One of the answers you'd almost certainly come up with is "variety." Another is "individuality." A third would be "change." Just look around you. The variety of life and nature on this planet alone is astounding. The number of individual beings is uncountable, each one unique in its way and ever-changing. We are immersed in change.

If these qualities are valued by a creator, by Consciousness, then perhaps the recognition of "non-duality" as the ultimate in spiritual awareness—a concept woven into religions from Hinduism, Buddhism, and Taoism through various branches of Western esotericism and mysticism—stops short not only of what is possible but of what is desirable. Maybe Consciousness, aware of itself in its totality, in its oneness, in its non-duality, became dual, became both Self and Other, to create, to expand into the ever-changing possibility of individuality.

That would be quite a challenge—to explore individual creation in the breadth and depth of all possibility. What happens when we lose sight of the oneness in our pursuit of individualism? What happens when creative impulses conflict or come up against the limits of time and space? We're finding that out now, aren't we? Maybe even All That Is doesn't know what can be created as All That Is becomes more of Itself.

If there is an ultimate unity of Consciousness, consider that perhaps in creating the realm of time and space, Consciousness intended that we (as an integral part of that Consciousness) learn to create from within this reality of limits, not reject it as flawed or see it as a place of suffering and punishment to be left behind as soon as we can. Maybe we aren't here to eventually learn how to escape this physical world, to "rejoin with the Source," or live forever strumming harps in heaven, but to create within this realm an infinitely inventive, imaginative, expressive world of joy, love, and wonder, aware of a larger reality, but intrigued and enchanted by the possibilities of this one.

Perhaps the suffering and pain we experience here is the result of choices made from a limited point of view, a consequence of having free will and the ability to create but limited awareness of our own abilities and powers. What if we can change that point of view, change those choices, instead of seeking to escape the consequences? Perhaps we are here to create while expanding our sense of self, not spend our lives longing to return to some painless state of relinquishing individuality in order to rejoin the Source. (Let me make clear here that I am not saying the suffering in this world is in any way the "fault" of those suffering. What I am saying is that we are involved in a creative endeavor in which we affect and are affected by each other, the environment, and circumstance, and we have far more power than we currently realize to change the world.)

So when we connect with Consciousness, with All That Is, when we slip free of our individual awareness and experience an expanded reality of oneness with the Absolute in what is often known as a "peak experience," then we may only be halfway on our journey. If Consciousness is ultimately creative, then perhaps we have the choice to experience individuality within time and space while consciously connected to a larger reality. Perhaps we were meant to forget and then remember, and that forgetting—with all the problems that entails—may be a necessary first step to this particular creative endeavor of Consciousness.

Given the state of our world, though, perhaps we have forgotten too much.

We are individuals; we exist within this physical realm. This much we know. To see our lives as some sort of Divine punishment or test or a "wheel of karma" from which we want to "break free" seems to me to be a poor response to this extraordinary gift of life. How might this world change if we were to honor each life on Earth as a gift and a creative challenge?

I, Me, Mine

Who am I?

This is the classic question asked by most of the Eastern religions—Hinduism, Buddhism, Taoism, and all their offshoots and branches. The question has been pondered in meditation for millennia. If reincarnation and/or consciousness beyond physical form exists (as these religions believe), then I am not bound by the externals of this lifetime, my body or my brain. I am not my thoughts, though my thoughts are mine. I am not my emotions, though my emotions are mine. So who the hell am I?

Some religions, notably Buddhism, see the sense of individuality as an illusion. Buddhism is a religion of great depth and variety, and Buddhist schools differ on the meaning of "no-self," and the path to liberation. But a basic point of agreement between the schools is the concept of self and soul as impermanent and ultimately an illusion. Enlightenment is a state of awareness that has no subject and no object.

Others, such as Hinduism (another religion of great depth and variety) and Taoism (more a profound philosophy than an actual religion) do postulate a self or soul but see it as part of a oneness—Brahman or Tao—and consider enlightenment, or full awareness of one's inseparability from that oneness, to be the goal of religious practice.

It may well be that individuality is an illusion, but (as Einstein noted about reality) it is a very persistent one and worth spending some time considering. I think the best way to consider it is in meditation. If you don't already have a meditation practice, this may be a good time to start one. We'll be looking at different meditation practices throughout the book, with, of course, further reading for you. Let's start with discursive meditation.

Discursive Meditation Exercise

Discursive meditation is a type of meditation that relies on analysis and logical thought. Set aside a few minutes a day for this practice and stick with it for at least a few months. See where it takes you. You can use this type of meditation to ponder any question, but to start, you might want to consider the question "Who am I?"

Don't aim to answer it so much as explore it. Start with the obvious: "Am I my body?" You may have a real sense that you *are* more than your body but aren't sure how that can be. Or perhaps you've had or known someone who has had an "out of body experience" and wondered about who it was that went out of the body. Perhaps your religious upbringing or life experiences left you with a conviction that you have an immortal soul, and you can't seem to shake that idea. Particularly if you believe in reincarnation, your answer to the question is likely to be no.

But your body is certainly yours. Perhaps your body is a creation of your Greater Self, the self that is aware of multiple incarnations? But then why would our selves create problems like ill health and birth defects? Maybe it's a question of Self having to create within certain limits of time and space and karmic limitations of which we—the incarnate self—are unaware? There is much to consider here.

You may come up with other answers—and other questions, such as "Am I my thoughts?" "Am I my emotions?" "How does my work define who I am?" "How do the choices I make define me?" You may want to do some research into how other people have answered similar questions. It's helpful to write in your journal on this topic.

Eventually, you may come to the conclusion that while you are possessed of a body, thoughts, emotions, etc., they do not define you. But they are yours. You may find it impossible to define exactly who you are, but if you continue with this contemplation, you will eventually begin to feel a core sense of self that is there whether you can define it or not.

Keep in mind that the point of this exercise should be to strengthen your sense of self, not erase it. By defining who you are, by considering that you are a nexus of Consciousness, that you have a Greater Self whose awareness spans lifetimes, by developing a rational framework for your own identity as an individual here on Earth who is also connected to a larger, timeless reality, you strengthen your presence and effectiveness in physical reality, and open to possibilities of expanding your consciousness into a larger reality.

Focusing Meditation Exercise

In addition to letting your reasoning mind chew on the question, you might also try a more experiential form of meditation. Sit quietly, eyes closed, and focus on your breathing for a moment. Let your breath soften and expand. As you inhale, say or think "I." As you exhale, say or think "am." Continue repeating "I am" with each breath. Let yourself experience your reality within time and space, as well as your connection with a Greater Self. You won't be able to force this experience or think your way into it. Just set an intent and expand your awareness. If your mind runs off with you—and it will—gently bring it back each time to focus on the phrase "I am." The only way you can do this wrong is by worrying about doing it wrong.

If neither of these meditations suit you—or even if they do—please take some time to explore other methods and the ideas behind meditation. You can start by reading books or taking classes, either online or in person. Whatever sort of meditation you're doing, set aside at least twenty minutes or so a day to practice. We'll cover altars in a later chapter, but honor this process by finding a place where you feel comfortable and safe, and where there will be no distractions. Lighting a candle when you do this will help you focus.

Eventually, as you work with these exercises, your sense of your current self and of your Greater Self should become stronger. You'll develop a solid sense of self-awareness, a base camp from which you can venture out to explore other realms of consciousness, knowing you can always find your way back. Though it's unlikely, if you begin feeling as though you are losing your sense of self, stop mediating and find someone to talk to about what's going on, preferably a therapist who understands and practices meditation.

While it's important to follow your train of thought and inner experience where it leads, at the end of meditations like these, remind yourself that no matter where your questions lead you, you experience yourself as an individual, you have a body, and you have agency in the material world. Some will suggest that this sense of self is an illusory state, which may well be the case. But here we are in this persistent illusion, and I think we are better served by strengthening our sense of self rather than relinquishing it. We can and should work on linking back to Consciousness, but we needn't dissolve into it.

As we expand our conscious awareness, we develop a greater understanding of our connections to Source and to each other. But relationship demands two entities, and defining who we are is the first step in relating well to both the world of spirit and to the outer world.

Nonetheless, it is important to realize that we are not, at our essence, any of the ephemeral, ever-changing things we identify with in physical reality. We are not our body, our brain, our thoughts, our likes and dislikes, our emotions. But all those things belong to us, spring from our essence, and create the "I" that interacts with other individuals. As you work with these ideas, you'll find that you come to an experiential sense of "I am" that will center and ground you in your unique, creative life. Developing this self is your mission ... should you decide to accept it.

Self-Acceptance

It's impossible to change if we can't be honest with ourselves. You probably wouldn't be reading this book if you were perfectly satisfied with your current life, so change is what you're after, right? But if you're afraid you won't measure up, afraid you'll find out something about yourself you don't like, afraid to face the trauma that you bottled up inside because you were too young to deal with it when it happened, afraid you'll be rejected, attacked, or abandoned by others, maybe even by "God," even if those fears are subconscious, then you might be a little resistant to change. Understandably so.

Fear makes us freeze in place. Also, many fears are imposed on us by our culture, and it's difficult to even recognize, much less change, emotions and ideas that are embedded in the cultural matrix. But we must learn to do exactly that—recognize and change problematic and disharmonious patterns within ourselves and at least recognize and disentangle ourselves from the ones within our culture.

The way we overcome the fear-based resistance, open to what life brings us, and use it as inspiration for our creativity is by learning to accept and love ourselves. Can you take it as a given, at least intellectually, that you are a worthy person, and you are doing the best you can in the moment?

It's obvious that you are searching for a better way, and you know there is one because you've listened to the voice of your soul. (Why else would you be reading this book?) The first step to self-acceptance is recognizing that you are a seeker. You know there is more to life and you want to find it. What do you seek? Joy? Love? Connection? Creative expression? Someone who seeks these things is a worthy person. Get used to it. Make a point of remembering it. Meditate on it. You are worthy.

Sure, we've all caused harm—and been harmed—at some point in our lives, and it's important to be aware of what happened and how it affected everyone involved. But carrying around blame, anger, and/or self-hatred does nothing to change the situation and keeps us frozen in our pain. Most, if not all, of the evil we find in this world stems from underlying fears—fears of separation, abandonment, annihilation, and pain. Too often, these fears overwhelm people, leading them to act in ways that cause harm.

The way out of this conundrum begins with actively learning to love and honor every part of ourselves. We can't change what's around us if we can't change what's within us. We can't use the gifts of our free will and creative abilities to create change in the world if our psyche is being fed a toxic brew of self-doubt, self-blame, and even self-hatred.

I see these harmful attitudes all the time in my clients and continue to deal with them in myself. It's the work of a lifetime to overcome imprinted negativity. People are frequently unaware of many of the negative opinions they hold of themselves—opinions usually formed in childhood. They project an image of confidence and competence that may or may not be supported by the facts, and focus their attention on the image, covering up their pain with a superficial layer of carefully manufactured "self-esteem." They also frequently carry a belief that criticism and punishment are inducements to improve, and so criticize and punish not only others, but themselves in their own thoughts. (That belief, by the way, is tightly woven into our culture. It's also been thoroughly disproven by psychology and neuroscience.)

To change these attitudes, we must consciously decide to create a pattern of true self-acceptance, not veneers of smug "self-esteem" we can hide behind, or fake humility that serves the purpose of keeping us safe from criticism, or any of the other facades we put up to avoid dealing with our pain and self-doubt. A good way to begin establishing this pattern is by using discursive meditation to think it through or by searching your heart for the evidence that you are worthy, loved, and capable of loving.

Watch your self-talk, what you say to yourself in your head. When you start beating yourself up for something, stop and look at it from a different perspective. Recognize that you have faults, and you are working on changing yourself. Yes, it's important to take responsibility for your mistakes and make necessary reparations, but first, you have to admit them—at least to yourself. If you make a habit of beating yourself up when you make a mistake, then there's a part of you that's going to try to deny your mistakes just to avoid the self-inflicted pain.

Crazy, isn't it? But most of us do this. Recognize that beating yourself up not only doesn't help, it makes things worse. So stop doing it! Develop an affirmation[10] like "I am a worthy and caring person," or "I love and I am loved" to help switch your thinking to a more positive focus when you realize your inner voice is being less than helpful. (You'll learn more about this in the thought-tracking meditation in chapter 6.)

You made a mistake. Ask yourself what's *realistically* the worst that can happen as a result. (No drama, OK?) Ask yourself if apologies or reparations are in order. Ask yourself which of your personal values you disregarded in

---

10. Affirmations have gotten a bad rap. Used mindlessly, they are futile and pointless. Used with clear intention and focus, they can help you make magic.

making this mistake and how you can avoid making similar mistakes in the future. All of these trains of thought are vastly more productive than "I'm an idiot! Why did I do that?! I always screw things up!" (or however your self-abnegation script reads). You accept what is past and change the future by changing your attitudes, thoughts, and beliefs in the present.

Clearly, this business of learning to accept and love yourself is a complex topic, and an important one. Stopping negative thought patterns is just a start. I've listed a number of books in the resources section that will help you learn to identify the negative patterns of thought and belief that are restricting your personal growth and development. But it's important to note something about any method of self-inquiry—*if you have trauma in your past, particularly in childhood, then actively working on changing yourself, on becoming more aware of your habitual patterns of thought and emotion, can bring up buried memories, beliefs, thoughts, and feelings that are difficult to deal with. If you have trauma in your past, you may want some help in dealing with the ongoing effects.* Finding a therapist is best, but it's important to find the right one, and they can be unaffordable for some. At the very least, read one or two of the books on developmental trauma I've listed at the end of this chapter. Working consciously with past trauma, while difficult and painful, is unavoidable if you want to eliminate problematic patterns in your life. It is also ultimately one of the most rewarding things you can do to improve your life.

Pitfalls on the Path

There are some common pitfalls on the spiritual path—states of mind and approaches to situations that lead us away from the experience of spirituality into a delusional state where we mistake the trappings of spirituality for the real thing and then use those trappings to avoid working on our neuroses and experiencing difficult emotions. Few of us will avoid these pitfalls—the best we can do is recognize when we are in a pit, figure out how to extract ourselves, and get back on the path. Eventually, we'll learn to recognize most of those pits so we can walk around them instead of falling in.

My first encounter with these ideas came through a book called *Cutting Through Spiritual Materialism* by Tibetan Buddhist lama Chögyam Trungpa, who defined the problem thusly:

Walking the spiritual path properly is a very subtle process; it is not something to jump into naively. There are numerous side-tracks which lead to a distorted, ego-centered version of spirituality; we can deceive ourselves into thinking we are developing spiritually when instead we are strengthening our egocentricity through spiritual techniques. This fundamental distortion may be referred to as *spiritual materialism*.[11]

Though I am not Buddhist and found much to disagree with in Trungpa's book, his explanation of spiritual materialism nailed many of the problems of emotional avoidance, psychological compartmentalization, and self-deception that plague spiritual seekers, leading them to substitute material achievements for experiences of a deeper reality because of a reluctance to face their own inner fears and neuroses. (Interestingly, Trungpa, like so many other spiritual teachers, fell into quite a few pits himself during his rather brief life. Understanding the problem does not exempt one from having to grapple with it.)

Later, when I began to study the work of psychologist C. G. Jung, I found that he and Trungpa were using the same word—ego—rather differently, but were describing a universal problem. Buddhism and Western psychology come at ego from differing approaches. Buddhism is based in a core philosophy of the oneness of all, of transcendent Consciousness that the seeker must learn to experience and then embody, learning the nature of suffering in the process and recognizing how suffering is tied in to the "illusion" of the ego. Western psychology comes from a more practical view that prioritizes healing from mental and emotional disturbances and sees the ego as a necessary, if often problematic, component of the psyche. But both Buddhism and Western psychology explore ways of changing consciousness by breaking through illusions of the mind to a clearer understanding of reality.

Jung's concept of the shadow (a part of our psyche that is not conscious that we reject as part of our whole self for a variety of reasons) and the accompanying concept of psychological projection (seeing what one cannot face in oneself projected onto other people) struck me as related to Trungpa's

11. Chögyam Trungpa, *Cutting Through Spiritual Materialism* (Boulder: Shambala Publications, 1973), 3.

concept of spiritual materialism resulting from the seeker's desire to numb pain and avoid suffering.

My understanding of pitfalls on the spiritual path all began to come together for me when I read about something called "spiritual bypassing," a term coined by psychotherapist and Buddhist teacher John Welwood back in the 1980s to describe a psychological defense mechanism that defends our ego-centered reality from the intrusion of anything that might threaten our egoic defenses and inner fears. Here's Welwood's description of the problem:

> In this way, involvement in spiritual teachings and practices can become a way to rationalize and reinforce old defenses. For example, those who need to see themselves as special will often emphasize the specialness of their spiritual insight and practice, or their special relation to their teacher, to shore up a sense of self-importance. Many of the "perils of the path"—such as spiritual materialism (using spiritual ideas for personal gain), narcissism, inflation (delusions of grandiosity), or groupthink (uncritical acceptance of group ideology)—result from trying to use spirituality to shore up developmental deficiencies.[12]

I'd seen that dynamic at work in myself and many others, especially during the years when I owned a metaphysical bookstore, spending a large portion of my days talking with customers about the questions and problems that had arisen for them on their spiritual path. So I began looking closely at these ideas, exploring my own shadow and "developmental deficiencies," and looking at concepts of ego both in Western psychology and Eastern spiritualities. I noted how easy it was to fall into these overly defensive psychological stances and delusional beliefs that seemed comforting but were simply avoidant.

Particularly in our Western culture where individual development is emphasized, spiritual pitfalls tend to manifest around issues of ego and self-expression. I have come to believe that ego, properly understood and integrated into the whole self, is a feature, not a bug. It is also a necessity for

---

12. John Welwood, *Toward a Psychology of Awakening: Buddhism, Psychotherapy, and the Path of Personal and Spiritual Transformation* (Boulder: Shambala Publications, 2000), 12–13.

living life within the physical plane. Ego has a job in the overall organization of our psyches and that job is to manage physical reality for us, to make certain limited decisions, and instigate actions in response to the outer world in line with the vision, directions, and boundaries set by the CEO—our Greater Self. Ideally, ego has an upper-management position with some power, but not the ultimate say-so. Ego, when it's assigned its proper job and not allowed to run the company ("Your Life, Inc."), is our friend. It assesses what's going on in outer reality and suggests strategies to deal with it.

But when the ego is running things, when it sits at the CEO's desk and starts making the kind of decisions only the CEO should make, that's when we see the overweening sense of self-importance that is what most people mean when they say someone is "egotistical" or "has an ego the size of a house." When ego is running things, we become overly conscious of how we appear to others, we compare ourselves to others, and we require outside admiration and affirmation because there is no underlying solid sense of self. We are anxious and fearful and often hide that fear and anxiety, even from ourselves. Often, fear influences us to put the ego in charge and listen to what it tells us to do, ignoring messages from our Greater Self. Ego puts a lot of stock in appearances because it's usually trying to cover up underlying shame and insecurities. It doesn't know how to heal shame—we need our Greater Self to help with that. Ego can only cover it up. Ego goes for control because it lacks vision, perspective, and understanding.

When the ego is making decisions for which it has neither the experience nor the information required, it's doing a job it's not qualified for. It will hijack our journey on our spiritual and magical path if we don't stay aware of the goals of our Greater Self for this lifetime. (And if you're wondering what the goals of your Greater Self are for this lifetime, astrology is one of the best tools I've found to help you answer that question.)

A lot of people fall into these traps of layering a new "spiritual" identity over their old, dysfunctional ones, and quite a few of these trapped people call themselves spiritual teachers. We need to be able to recognize some of these spiritual pitfalls in others as well as ourselves because it's easy to fall into these traps and they can cause a lot of damage, particularly when someone puts themselves forward as a teacher. There are some conversational and behavioral gambits that are a dead giveaway.

One indication of spiritual bypassing is relentless positivity. When someone consistently denies any negative emotions, focuses on "purity" or "cleansing," or insists that all you need to do to improve your life is repeat positive affirmations ad nauseum, you're almost certainly dealing with someone whose fear of anything "negative" is being repressed and denied as they layer what they believe is "spiritual" over their fear. But we must integrate the shadow and bring those hidden aspects of ourselves into the light and either integrate or transform them. Denying the negative aspects of our lives only perpetuates the negativity instead of healing it.

We also see ego run rampant as a manifestation of spiritual bypassing, especially in Western cultures. When the ego has put itself in charge, there's a fragile sense of self that needs shoring up, and people driven by ego will take every opportunity to extol the superiority of their path, drop broad hints about being "enlightened," or "saved," or "powerful." If they don't tell you outright, they imply that their way is the only way. It's fine to discuss the pros and cons of various philosophies—in fact, that is an important part of determining one's own path. It's the cutting remarks and the condescending attitude that flag the difference between thoughtful analysis and the need to feel "better than."

Another big hint that someone has fallen into one of these pitfalls is the lack of a sense of humor. Humor is one quality I've noticed that all the truly spiritually awakened people I have met (or read about) share. It can run the gamut from subtle and self-deprecating through obvious farce and slapstick, but they all have a keen sense of humor and are able to laugh at themselves and laugh with the world.

Recognizing spiritual bypassing in others, especially those we may be looking to as teachers, can, ironically, cause us to fall into the same trap ourselves. It's easy to avoid dealing with our own issues by denying any negativity or looking down our noses at a self-styled "guru," "high priestess," "shaman," or "adept," certain that we, having recognized another's bypassing and projection, are therefore free of it ourselves. But when we find ourselves judging others, we need to look carefully at our own underlying motivations and try to find some compassion. We can't put ourselves in another's mind. It may be that this person who is so sure they are a teacher for the ages is sitting on more pain than you've ever experienced in your life and is having a tough time dealing with it.

It's telling that this person chose spirituality to bolster their sense of self instead of, say, getting an advanced academic degree or jumping on the corporate fast-track because they do feel the call of spirit. Yes, some are downright sociopathic, but for the most part, underneath the insecurities, people who fall into this trap are curious, creative, and looking for a path to the larger reality they know exists.

You certainly want to avoid being overly influenced by these people and, if you are in a position to do so, to minimize the harm they cause others. But finding some compassion in your heart for them may help them find their own path to healing and will certainly help you find yours.

As you consider your reasons for pursuing a spiritual path, keep a close eye on your own behavior. When you find yourself hyping or defending your religion, philosophy, or beliefs, pointing to your own advanced spiritual state (often with an overlay of false modesty), or losing your sense of humor, then check in with your fears, check in with your sense of self-worth (or lack thereof), and make a note of how connected you feel to the love and power of spirit in this moment (hint: probably not very). If you've done the work of learning to love yourself, of connecting to your Greater Self, then you'll be able to honestly recognize that it's simply ego sitting at the CEO's desk again. Send ego back to its own office and open the door to let your Greater Self back in.

Deciding Who You Are

One of the best ways to put your Greater Self back in charge is simply to sit down and decide who you want to be. What does the person you want to be value? What do they believe? How does this person act and react in various situations? Who do they love? As you ask yourself these questions, and perhaps write about them in your journal, the answers you come up with will hopefully be guided by your Greater Self. Then you can work on bringing your thoughts and actions in line with those of the person you want to be.

Tools for the Journey of Self-Discovery

There are a number of tools that can help you in your process of self-discovery. Meditation is one, and which we have already explored. Astrology, of course, is one of my favorites, since, as a professional astrologer, I've devoted much of my life to its study and practice. The astrology chart is your soul's blueprint for this lifetime. It shows what your plans are for this time around, highlights the past life and karmic issues you are dealing with, details your strengths, maps the challenges you've laid out for yourself in this incarnation, and helps you keep on track and in tune with your soul. I've listed a couple of self-help style astrology books below, but it's a complex subject and I suggest getting your chart interpreted by a good professional astrologer at least once.

Tarot is another excellent tool, both for self-discovery and for developing your intuition. Read a couple of the books below, get yourself a deck, and learn by pulling one to three cards a day, asking a simple, open-ended question like, "What do I need to focus on today?" Then journal about it in the evening. One caveat—don't try to do predictive readings for yourself at first. You need experience to be able to read the future for yourself accurately, and it's too easy to scare yourself silly trying. But for insights into current issues and advice on how to deal with them, tarot is unparalleled.

It's a good idea to write down your readings, which brings me to journaling, one of the best tools for self-discovery. Some people like to journal daily, some, like me, are more slapdash about it. But it's really helpful to first get thoughts out of your head and on to paper and, second, to have those thoughts to look back over in the future when you have some emotional distance. It helps you evaluate your life, explore solutions, and objectively assess situations.

And let's not forget magic and ritual. When you ritually state your intent to the universe, the universe replies, bringing events, insights, and synchronicities into your life that make clear what and how you need to change to change your intent into reality. But we'll get into more depth about ritual and practice in a bit. Right now, let's celebrate Imbolc!

Resources

Thich Nhat Hanh and Vo-Dihn Mai, *The Miracle of Mindfulness: An Introduction to the Practice of Meditation* (Boston: Beacon Press, 1996).

David Frawley, *Vedantic Meditation: Lighting the Flame of Awareness* (Berkeley: North Atlantic Books, 2014).

Evelyn Underhill, *Mysticism: A Study in Nature and Development of Spiritual Consciousness* (New York: E.P. Dutton, 1961).

Harriet Lerner, Ph.D., *The Dance of Fear: Rising Above Anxiety, Fear, and Shame to Be Your Best and Bravest Self* (New York: HarperPerennial, 2005).

Jane Roberts, *The Nature of Personal Reality: A Seth Book* (New York: Bantam Books, 1978).

Tara Brach, *Radical Acceptance: Embracing Your Life With the Heart of a Buddha* (New York: Bantam Books, 2004).

Nathaniel Branden, *The Six Pillars of Self-Esteem* (New York: Bantam Books, 1995).

Laurence Heller, Ph.D., and Aline Psyd Lapierre, *Healing Developmental Trauma: How Early Trauma Affects Self-Regulation, Self-Image, and the Capacity for Relationship* (Berkeley: North Atlantic Books, 2012).

Bessel van der Kolk, M.D., *The Body Keeps the Score: Brain, Mind, and Body in the Healing of Trauma* (London: Penguin Books, 2014).

Peter A. Levine and Ann Frederick, *Waking the Tiger: Healing Trauma* (Berkeley: North Atlantic Books, 1997).

S. Kelley Harrell and Christina Pratt, *Gift of the Dreamtime—Awakening to the Divinity of Trauma* (Fuquay-Varina, Soul Intent Arts, 2012).

Chogyam Trungpa, *Cutting Through Spiritual Materialism* (Boulder: Shambala Publications, 1973).

John Welwood, *Toward a Psychology of Awakening: Buddhism, Psychotherapy, and the Path of Personal and Spiritual Transformation* (Boulder: Shambala Publications, 2002).

Ivo Dominguez, Jr., *Practical Astrology for Witches and Pagans* (Newbury port: Weiser Books, 2016).

Demetra George and Douglas Bloch, *Astrology for Yourself: How to Understand And Interpret Your Own Birth Chart* (Lake Worth: Ibis Press, 2006).

Mary Greer, *Tarot for Yourself A Workbook for Personal Transformation* (Newburyport: New Page Books, 2nd Edition 2002).

Janet Conner, *Writing Down Your Soul: How to Activate and Listen to the Extraordinary Voice Within* (Newburyport: Conari Press, 2009).

Veda Vyasa and Swami Vijnanananda (trans.), *The Devî Gita: Song of the Goddess* (n.p., 2011).

Erwin Schrodinger, *What Is Life? With Mind and Matter and Autobiographical Sketches* (Cambridge: Cambridge University Press, 2012).

Online

Jason Miller's Take Back Your Mind online class, http://www.strategicsorcery .net/courses/take-back-your-mind/.

CHAPTER SIX
Imbolc—The Winter/ Spring Midpoint

The days lengthen as we move from Winter Solstice toward Imbolc—the midpoint between winter and spring. We, too, begin to emerge from the darkness and the inward focus of winter to renew our contract with life.

Even when we live in a big city surrounded by buildings and technology, there's an atavistic part of us that keeps track of things like light and temperature. It draws us inward when it's dark and cold, then gets us moving out into the world again as the light and warmth increase. Thanks to electricity, we no longer have to read by candlelight or huddle in front of a fire to stay warm, but our ancestral brain never loses its connection with the planet and still pays close attention to the changing seasons. As the light increases, we are naturally moved to engage more with the world, spend more time outdoors and with others, and prepare for the increased activity of the upcoming warm months.

The traditional date for Imbolc is February 2; the astronomical midpoint is right around February 4. The word "Imbolc" is rooted in the language of Old Irish and means "in the belly." As with all the cross-quarter festivals, the symbolism is closely tied to agricultural realities. In this case, it's the time of lambing, when the ewes bring forth new life from their bellies.

Let me detour here for a moment into agricultural realities. One of the criticisms people often direct toward Wicca is that it's based in an older, agricultural way of life, and we don't live like that anymore. But the reality is that if you are eating anything at all, your life is based in agricultural realities.

Chapter Six

You may not have to feed the chickens, weed the vegetables, pick the fruit, or milk the cows, but that is all the more reason to acknowledge the people who do and the land that supports us. OK, back to the holiday.

Another name for this holiday is Candlemas, which is my favorite, since it echoes the returning light and speaks to a small flame held through the winter and the transformative magic of fire.

In a number of Pagan traditions, late winter is a time that is used for self-assessment, purification, transformation, and dedication or rededication to a spiritual path. As we prepare to engage more with the world, it's useful to ask ourselves, "Who do I want to be in the world? Who do I want to become? What is holding me back? What commitment is required from me to become that person? What old thoughts, beliefs, and habits do I need to shed to become who I want to be?" Once we've answered these questions—at least for the moment—we purify ourselves of any stagnant energy that is holding us back. Then, like a snake shedding its old skin, we can face this new cycle of life renewed and transformed.

One of the ways this holiday is celebrated is by blessing the candles that will be used for ritual throughout the year. Other celebrations include revering Bridget, goddess of healing, poetry, and the sacred fires of hearth and forge, who is associated with this holiday in Irish lore. Celebrations of the returning spring are also part of this time, for the light is growing and though we may not see the signs yet, under the snow life is stirring. Sap is running in the trees, and the ewes are giving birth to lambs.

This holiday falls in the sign of Aquarius, the sign of individuality, friends, groups, and social justice. Essentially, it covers the work that must be done to build a civilization, which encompasses but is more than simply a government and infrastructure. Aquarius believes a healthy civilization is driven and sustained by agreed upon ideas and ideals that enshrine individual rights and freedom for all while enabling individuals to work together in groups for the good of all. (You may have noticed that this goal is rather difficult to enact, but Aquarius will keep trying!)

Traditionally, in Ireland, Imbolc involved trips to holy wells and the associated magic, like clootie magic—tying a piece of cloth with your wish written on it to a tree by the well. There were also rituals of purification and blessing as well as offerings to spirits of nature and gods. In many Wiccan traditions, this is the time when rituals are done to dedicate to or initiate into a tradition or working group. It's a good time to reaffirm your dedication to your own spiritual path and reassess your connection to any groups you're involved with. What ways can you think of that you might celebrate this time of year? Here are some ideas.

—| KISS THE SKY |—

I'm putting the Kiss the Sky section first this time because there are some things you'll want to ponder before you do the Touch the Earth work.

Thought-Tracking Exercise

One of the best ways to get to know both yourself and your Greater Self better is to pay more attention to your thoughts. Where do your thoughts come from? Some of them appear to be in reaction to current events, both external and internal. Some just bubble up—or erupt—into your mind. Many of those will be from your subconscious, or your unconscious. Some will be from your soul or your Greater Self. And it's good to pay attention to all these thoughts as they arise. But it's also possible to harness your mind and learn to direct your thoughts. This is the work of the magician, and the place to begin your training is discovering where you are right now by paying attention to your habitual thought patterns.

Start by setting an alarm for three or four different times during the day—times when you're pretty sure you can take just a minute or two to shift your attention to this work. When the alarm rings, immediately note what you were just thinking, then trace your thoughts back as far as you can. Keep asking, "What was I thinking before that?"

As an example, let's say you're stuck in traffic driving from work to pick your child up at school when the alarm rings, and you're thinking, "The traffic around here just keeps getting worse." Before that? "Stopping at the cleaners is going to be a nightmare with all this traffic and I need to get Sally to soccer practice by 5:30." Before that? "I wish Jim would stop talking my ear off every time I walk past his desk—he's made me late again!"

Once you've identified your thoughts, take a moment to become aware of what kind of thoughts they are: Worried thoughts? Planning thoughts? Thoughts of appreciation? Are you in the moment, in the past, or in the future? Are you berating, blaming, or judging yourself or another? Then refocus your mind on the kind of thoughts you want to be having. Have a few short affirmations or prayers memorized that you can immediately call up. Think about what you are grateful for in your life, or simply bring your attention fully into the present moment (especially if you're driving!). Take a few aware, conscious breaths. See how long you can stay focused in the present as you bring your attention fully into the world around you.

You may not be able to get more than two or three thoughts back at first, but you'll find your recall improves with practice. You may choose to write them down immediately, later, or not at all. I suggest keeping a notebook with you, though, so you have a place to jot down anything you want to remember to write about more fully in your journal. You can also keep your affirmations and prayers written in the front or back so you can find them easily if you forget them. Try to get at least the gist of a few of your thoughts down in your journal—shoot for daily, but every few days will do. Note what you were thinking and how it aligned—or didn't—with the kind of thoughts you want to be thinking.

After you've been doing this for a while, you'll begin to see patterns and become more aware of how you use your mental energy. If you find yourself thinking a lot of blaming, judgmental, vengeful, or worried thoughts, you can be sure that you are carrying the energy of those thoughts around with you. You might want to dig a bit and see where they come from and if they are in line with the person you want to be. Ditto for thoughts of appreciation, hope, and love. You may find there are things you think about obsessively, and obsession is rarely helpful. We all learn problematic and negative patterns of thinking as we are growing up from our parents, teachers, friends, and other authority figures.

Whether your thoughts are currently helpful or problematic, don't blame yourself or pat yourself on the back—just be aware. You should particularly become aware of self-shaming and judgment. Shame is a feeling that is useful only in that it informs you that you have erred against your own values and need to bring the situation back into some kind of energetic balance. Energetic balance is *not* achieved by continually castigating yourself—you have more creative and positive ways of using your thought-energy.

Do your best to journal regularly, making notes of any insights you have into the patterns of thought you've noticed. You also might want to keep an ongoing list of your core values and beliefs then make a point of challenging them regularly. Core values and beliefs are those ideas by which you choose to live your life. They are solid, integrated into your being, and not subject to whims, but they are changeable. Consider that some probably need to be changed because we often hold conflicting values in our unconscious. These conflicting values and beliefs can cause all kinds of trouble for us until we make them conscious and release or integrate them. Paying attention to your thoughts and thought patterns will help you discover what is truly important to you, so you can calibrate your moral compass.

Why bother doing this exercise? Here are some of the benefits:

- To train and strengthen your mind, which is the source of all magic
- To consciously reset and realign your personal energy
- To identify and release negative patterns of thought
- To see more clearly how your thoughts are reflected in your daily life
- To clarify your core beliefs and values

Cleansing and Purification

Our culture carries a lot of baggage around those two words, so it's important to define our terms here. Just as we need to cleanse our physical bodies regularly, we also need to cleanse our minds and our auric/etheric bodies. But we must think carefully about what we are cleansing ourselves of, what we consider to be "pure." I've seen a lot of nonsense promulgated around those two words, from "clean" diets that deny the body its needed nourishment to "purity" being associated with virginity. So let's give some thought to what those words really mean.

There's a point of view that believes everything is holy, the universe is unfolding in its perfection just as it should, and we should "surrender" or "have faith." Personally, I don't buy it. I believe the universe is ultimately creative, and creativity is a messy business. I have to wonder if the people who say everything is holy have ever experienced or even read about the experiences of those who have been tortured or gang raped or have watched their child's brains dashed out against a rock by a soldier bent on death and destruction. These things happen. They are not holy. They are not perfection. They are not OK, and I, for one, will never "surrender" to a world that contains them.

Yes, there is a place from which we can see these things as an expression of our free will to create whatever we can imagine, a part of the process of exploring this world of time and space. We can gain knowledge of and take comfort in our soul's eternal existence as we explore the greater love and connection that is possible when we choose to move away from fear. We can experience our oneness with the universe and understand that those painful events, those terrible choices, are all held within that oneness. But that doesn't mean we should accept them. That doesn't mean we shouldn't try to create something better, to envision and manifest a world that is free of cruelty and savage brutality. (Whether or not it should or even can be free of suffering is another question you might want to consider at some point. The unavoidability of suffering is a core tenet of Buddhism and some other religions.)

I suggest that we need to cleanse and purify ourselves as a way of making and stating our choices, of saying, "I want this in my world, but not this other thing." Here's an example. I spent a number of years working as a volunteer rape crisis advocate, which involved getting a call, usually in the middle of the night, and driving to the hospital to sit with, advocate for, and hopefully offer some comfort to a someone who had just been raped. The thought-energies that are freely floating around a hospital are not very conducive to healing or peace of mind (understandably), and because the medical establishment doesn't have space for such a thing in its world view, this negativity and its effect on healing is not even acknowledged.

Sure, I could put up adamantine psychic shields, but then I wouldn't be able to connect energetically with the person I'm there to help. So I walk in there knowing that my personal energy is going to be impacted by a lot of painful, negative energy, particularly from my client. And I'm OK with that because I know I can help shift the energy around someone who needs help clearing the energy of violence and victimization from their own auric field and also needs an infusion of loving and caring energy.

I've trained to protect myself from these kinds of difficult energies in the moment, but I'm more focused on helping and protecting another, and when

I leave, some of it always seems to stick. But I can go home, take a salt bath, meditate, and ask my helping spirits for assistance in clearing my own auric field of any energy I was unable to release or transform at the time. That I do both the work and the cleansing speaks to my choice to do what I can to help create a world healed from violence and trauma. Violence and trauma are not holy. But we can use them to create a better world by acknowledging their part in the creative explorations of Consciousness, while at the same time releasing them to be transformed. Once cleansed of what we have chosen to release from our personal reality, then we affirm the world we do want by keeping our own personal energy in resonance with our dreams and visions.

So think carefully about what you are cleansing yourself of and why. It's important not to start channeling Lady Macbeth (cleanliness as an outlet for repressed guilt) or Howard Hughes. (Hughes was terrified of germs. Paranoia is not a good place to be.) Don't get obsessive about your state of psychic cleanliness, just attend to it regularly and occasionally ritually (more on that later) as you would brush your teeth and go for the occasional professional cleaning.

There are books at the end of this chapter about cleansing and protection, and there's information on a cleansing bath you can do in the Touch the Earth section. Read what calls to you and integrate a regular psychic/energetic cleansing routine into your daily life.

Affirmation of Dedication

This is a short, memorable phrase or prayer that you create as a meditative touchstone, a way of returning your consciousness to the remembrance of your spiritual aspirations and core values and reaffirming your commitment to them. (It's a good one to add to your stash of affirmations in your thought-tracking journal.)

You'll want to set aside a quiet evening or morning to do this work. Start by writing in your journal. Write on the ideas you've been contemplating about your personal relationship to the larger cosmos, your core values and beliefs, and the direction you want to take with your life. Remember any peak spiritual experiences you may have had. Think about what brings you joy. Spend some time with this process. Establish clearly what it is you desire so much that you are willing to dedicate yourself to attaining it in the year ahead. Have a clear picture in your mind of the outcome.

Perhaps the outcome is you being in a place of greater clarity about how the world works and what part consciousness and/or spirituality plays in it. Knowledge is a form of power in the world, and it can help us develop wisdom. You might dedicate to gaining knowledge. You can see it as an ideal that guides you and the human race to greater attainments. You might also dedicate to both wisdom and knowledge or wisdom through knowledge —whatever is significant and relevant to you personally.

Perhaps the outcome is you being in a place where you have found a meaningful, inspirational way of living in the world. A way of looking at life that brings expansion of awareness, greater emotional depth, and a deeper appreciation of life's extraordinary beauty. Then you can dedicate yourself to finding and following that path.

Perhaps you have co-religionists, others who believe as you do, and you wish to make a dedication to a group and the spiritual path/religion that you share. The point is that you have a vision of where you want to go and at least a rough map of the journey that will get you there. Then you make a formal commitment (certainly to yourself, perhaps to others as well) to that vision and that journey. Once you are clear on what you want to commit to, set aside a bit of time to do the exercise below.

⊣ TOUCH THE EARTH ⊢

The Purification Bath

After you've thought about what purification means to you, you can do a ritual of purification for yourself. Here's a simple one:

1. Clean your bathroom with focus and awareness that this is preparation for the sacred work you will be doing in it.

2. Prepare about 2 cups of strong tea made from a small handful each of any three of the following herbs:

   • Lemon Verbena

   • Hyssop

- Rosemary
- Sage
- Eucalyptus
- Parsley
- Chamomile

Strain the tea, then add it to a salt bath (1–2 cups of salt in the tub) or put the tea in a large bucket of salt water (1 cup salt in a 5-gallon bucket) and bring it into the shower with a pitcher.

3. Bring a blue, white, or natural beeswax candle and some sage, cedar, or other purifying incense into the bathroom. The candle can be a votive or a seven-day candle in glass. You'll want to burn it several times during the next six weeks while meditating and eventually let it burn all the way down, so choose the size with that in mind. If your time is at a premium, and/or you aren't at home a lot (you don't want to leave your burning candle unattended), go for the smaller votive. If you have time for longer meditations and spend plenty of time at home, go with the bigger one.

4. Holding the candle, speak to your Greater Self and/or your ancestors, any gods, or other spirit beings that you feel connected to. Tell them what you think you need to be purified of and ask for their help. Light the candle and incense.

5. Get in the bath/shower. If you are in a bath, soak at least ten minutes, ducking your head under the water at least three times. If that's not possible, use a pitcher to pour water over your head. If you are in the shower, let the water run over you, then turn the shower off and use the pitcher to pour the water from the bucket over you. Do this three times.

6. During the bath/shower, repeat the phrase "I release all negative and inharmonious energies from my life" (or something similar) several times. If you are taking a bath, drain the water. Whether bath or shower, finish up with a rinse in the shower, visualizing all that unwanted energy flowing down the drain, and also visualizing yourself being nourished and restored by the water.

7. Once you have dried off, pick the candle up and spend a few moments watching the flame. Let it take you to an aware and centered space. Now that the energetic barnacles and accretions are gone from your energetic field, let in the energy of fire, and allow it to enliven every cell. (Remember from chapter 4 that living cells produce photons—the elementary particle of light.)

8. As you watch the flame, sense your connection to your Greater Self, to the larger world of spirit, and see yourself invigorated and blessed by the living light while repeating your affirmation of dedication. Let the candle burn for a bit while you dress, then blow it out and put it on your altar, or someplace safe. In the upcoming weeks, when you want to clear your energy, light the candle, use the Tai Chi cleansing breath (below), then envision the candle flame enlivening your cells as you repeat your cleansing affirmation.

Tai Chi Cleansing Breath

There is a quick way of clearing your personal energy that is helpful to practice. I learned it first in a Tai Chi class. Once you've practiced it enough, you can just think your way through it if you're in a public place and need a quick clearing. It's a movement used in some schools of Tai Chi to release negative energy from the body and bring in new energy. If you can do this outdoors, so much the better.

- Stand with your feet about shoulder distance apart, arms at your side. Take a few deep breaths and settle into your body. Be aware of the earth below you, the sky above you.

- Turn your palms outward as you raise your arms over your head, inhaling. Imagine yourself inhaling fresh chi, or energy, and gathering it in with your arms.

- As your arms are directly overhead, palms facing each other, bend your elbows so your palms face the ground and fingertips face each other.

- Then bring your hands down in front of your body as far as you can (palms pointing down, fingertips pointing toward each other). Envision any old, stale, inharmonious energy being pushed out through your feet into the Earth. (No, you aren't harming the Earth, the Earth will transform the energy.)

Repeat two more times.

Cleansing Fire

A quick way to clear the energy of a room is to burn an epsom salt/alcohol fire in the room. This is a clean-burning fire (no smoke) that you can use indoors. Here's what you'll need:

- A fireproof container. And I do mean fireproof. This fire is smoke-free, but it generates real heat. I use a 6-inch cast-iron cauldron that stands on three short legs. I put this container on a heavy ceramic tile and make sure it is far away from anything flammable.
- A fireproof lid you can use to cover the fire if it gets out of hand. You shouldn't need it, but have it anyway. I've never had a problem with this kind of fire, but you might want to have a fire extinguisher nearby as well.
- ¼ to 1 cup of Epsom salts, depending on the size of the container
- An equal amount (by volume) of 90 percent isopropyl (rubbing) alcohol (make sure you get the 90 percent, not the 70 percent)
- Fireplace matches or a long lighter
- Optional: one to three essential oils good for clearing, such as eucalyptus, rosemary, or sage

Here's how to do it:

1. Set up the container on a heat-proof surface near the center of the room. Take all precautions to make sure nothing flammable is nearby. The fire won't escape the container, but it will flare upward. Make sure the lid is in easy reach.
2. Put a small amount of Epsom salts in the bottom of the container. I use ½ cup in a 6-inch diameter and 4-inch deep cast iron cauldron. Add the alcohol and several drops of essential oils if you are using them.

3. Open at least one window or door in the room, at least a crack, even if it is the dead of winter. All that stuff you're clearing needs a way to get out.

4. Standing well back and using a long match or lighter, touch the alcohol with the fire. It should light up immediately.

5. Stay in the room as the fire burns out. Meditate on the fire transforming stagnant energy and the fresh energy filling the room. It will take a while to burn down, depending on how much alcohol you used to start with. When the container has cooled (and not before!), rinse it out, sending the remaining Epsom salts down the drain. You may need to soak it for a while—the Epsom salts will be hardened and crusty.

Grounding and Centering

Grounding and centering is a key practice for magic, meditation, and prayer, but it's also good just for stress relief and getting through daily life. There are lots of different techniques. Here's one that is fairly simple.

At first, what you are doing will seem entirely imaginary. But you are actually moving energy, building and sensing real energetic constructs. As you learn more about energy (starting in the next chapter) and continue this practice you'll find your sense of what's happening on more subtle levels will grow.

Ideally, you'll do this exercise outside, but realistically, you won't always be able to, so just know that you are still connected to the ground through the building you are in.

To ground yourself, stand in a comfortable, balanced stance, feet shoulder distance apart. Be aware of Earth beneath your feet, the stars above you.

Take three cleansing breaths, sweeping your arms overhead, palm up (gathering fresh energy), then down in front of you, palms down (pushing out old, stale energy). Inhale as you move your arms up, exhale as you push them down. Then resume your balanced stance.

Bring your awareness fully into the present. Sense what you are seeing, hearing, feeling, smelling, and tasting. Notice your breath, and let it move into your belly. Spend a few moments just paying attention to your breath, allowing it to reach a natural rhythm.

Imagine a cord of energy connecting you to the core of the planet itself through the base of your spine. The energy flows both ways—into you from the Earth, through your spine, infusing you with strong, warm, vital energy, into the Earth from you, taking away any stale or negative energy.

Now imagine a beam of light coming down from the stars that enters through the top of your head (the fontanel, or soft spot on a baby's head) and runs down your spine, where it joins with the energy that is rising from the Earth. Let the energy flow through you as you stand balanced between earth and sky.

(If you saw the movie *Avatar*, you'll remember how the Na'vi would join with other beings through the tentacles on the end of their queue. That's how I visualize the energy from Earth and stars coming together within my spine. Then the combined energy infuses the whole body. If you didn't see the film, search "Na'vi queue connection" for some YouTube videos of the process. If it works for you, use it, but if not, just discover your own way of visualizing the two strands of energy.)

Sweep your arms up over your head again then bring your palms together in front of your heart center and draw your feet together. Sense the small movements of your body as you find your balance point. You will probably notice that your balance is dependent on small motions of your body as you constantly recenter yourself. But there is a center still point.

Now repeat an affirmation or prayer. "I stand centered between Earth and stars" is fine, or you can come up with something more elaborate and/or personalized. Then take a deep breath and you're done.

Do this at least daily. Eventually, you'll be able to do it just in your mind, which can be very useful in the middle of a workday when you're feeling stressed out, and you may find just doing a quick mental version several times a day is helpful. But do the actual physical motions as often as you can. Just because you can do it in your mind doesn't mean you should ignore the physical exercise. We are in our bodies for a reason.

The Dedication Meditation.

Some of you already have a sense of affiliation with a spiritual path, some of you are seeking a path, and others of you are just trying to decide if you want anything to do with this spiritual stuff or not. So, I can't tell you exactly what to dedicate to. That's up to you. It can simply be to an open-minded exploration of spirituality, to studying a particular path or religion (which will likely have its own dedication ceremonies) or even just dedicating to finding the spiritual path that is right for you.

Once you have a clear idea of what you are dedicating to, you'll want to take some time to experience it, to make it real for you, not just an idea in your head. Sit down in a comfortable place where you won't be disturbed and light a candle and maybe some incense. (Doing this first will directly affect your experience of this exercise. Candlelight and incense are neuroactive, not just symbolic.) Take a few deep breaths. Let yourself look at the candle flame, bringing your awareness fully into the present moment. Focus on your breathing for a little while, simply releasing any thoughts that come up and returning to the present moment.

Once you've settled in, think about what it would *feel* like to encounter the outcome that you desire, this goal you have for your life journey. What emotions would you experience? What would it be like to wake up every morning and face the day with enthusiasm and expectation? With joy and compassion? Without fear? Bring the outcome you want down from your head to imbue your heart as well. Imagine the emotions—joy, love, contentment, inspiration, connection with others—that this outcome will bring you.

Let yourself sit with these feelings for a while. Imagine them. Explore them. Release any thoughts of "this can't happen," or "something's bound to go wrong—it always does," or "I'll never be able to do this." While these thoughts need to be sourced and the underlying beliefs investigated and changed, now is not the time for that. Let them go (if writing them down helps you release them, grab your journal and then come back to this exercise). Focus on the feelings you want. Remember times in your life when you have felt joy and love and connection. Concentrate on what you are dedicating to.

Now take the ideas and the feelings from your head and heart and let them sink into your gut. This is where you manifest them, bring them into this physical world. You should feel the focus of this energy in a spot around two inches below your belly button. (This is the *dan tien* of Chinese medicine and martial arts, the area of the second chakra of the Yogic arts of healing.) You don't need to understand the "how" of this—just hold the intention of bringing this new reality into existence. Sense the energy of your dedication manifesting in the world. Sit with this energy for a while. Sense the reservoir of energy at your core. Breathe fully.

Now sense the energy of what you are dedicating to resonating in your head, your heart, and your belly. Ask for a phrase of affirmation, a phrase, a prayer, or even a single word that will help you remember these thoughts, feelings, and sensations that you have just generated. A phrase that will encapsulate all of this and bring it back when you are in the middle of your crazy life and need to be reminded of what you are living for, what you are dedicated to. Ask your unconscious, or your Greater Self, or your helping spirits, or your ancestors, or your gods. Or just ask the universe.

The phrase may come to you as you are doing the exercise, or it may come to you at some point over the next few days. It may be something original to you, or it may be from a poem, song, or prayer that is meaningful to you. Don't worry if you don't get it right away. You've done the work, and the results will come. Don't over think this, and don't fall into perfectionism. You can always change the phrase if your first effort turns out to be not quite right. Just let one come to you or make one up over the next few days.

Before you end this exercise, you might want to journal a bit about it. Then thank any of the nonphysical beings you have asked to help you, and blow out the candle.

Repeat your affirmation regularly. It will help you stay on the path you have chosen.

Check In with Others

Organize a group or set up a ritual of connection for a group you are already in, or sign up to do some volunteer work for a non-profit group.

Resources

Carl F. Neal, *Imbolc: Rituals, Recipes & Lore for Brigid's Day* (St. Paul: Llewellyn Publications, 2015).

Amber K and Azrael Arynn K, *Candlemas: Feast of Flames* (St. Paul: Llewellyn Publications, 2001).

Khi Armand, *Clearing Spaces: Inspirational Techniques to Heal Your Home* (New York: Sterling Ethos, 2017).

David Salisbury, *A Mystic Guide to Cleansing & Clearing* (London: Moon Books, 2016).

Denise Linn, *Sacred Space: Clearing and Enhancing the Energy of Your Home* (New York: Wellspring/Ballantine, 2007).

Energy, Ritual, and Practice

W e've been considering some pretty wild ideas and you may be finding it hard to wrap your mind around some of them. How can anything exist that isn't physical? What does that even mean? If spiritual beings exist, where do they exist? If there are beings that exist outside of time and space, then is there even such a thing as "where" for them?

Spiritual practices help answer these questions because they bring speculation into the realm of experience. Remember that exploring the limits of Consciousness is going to involve reaching beyond our rational minds. Not because what is beyond our minds is necessarily irrational, but our minds are not yet evolved enough to understand the calculus of the universe. We're still working on basic math. Certainly, it's remarkably difficult for us to even conceptualize being without time and space, but the experiences of many meditators suggest that we can come into what Jane Robert's Seth often referred to as "the spacious present," the awareness of being beyond time.

Spring is a good time of year to develop or review your spiritual practices. These practices can cover the gamut from prayer and meditation through trancework, ritual, and magical workings, to physical practices designed to heal and strengthen our etheric bodies and shift consciousness through physical effort—such as certain styles of Yoga, dance, and martial arts.

These are practices that teach us to explore states of conscious awareness that are not as confined by time and space as our normal waking consciousness. We learn to use the dial on the radio that is our brain, moving beyond that golden oldies station, beyond the talk radio shows, beyond the idle chatter of the mind. We can learn to travel the airwaves freely, interact with other individual consciousnesses that are not tied to time and space, and get different perspectives of our life here on Earth. As we do that, we come to experience and understand our own existence outside of a physical body, outside of our daily thoughts and emotions. Spiritual practices lead to a greater understanding and control of the ultimate (and least understood) tool of science, the human mind, and then to an encounter with our soul and with spirit.

Spiritual practices also honor this remarkable world we live in, helping us connect fully to it. We can increase our influence and creative abilities within it through these practices. Through spiritual practice, we pattern the energy of our bodies and our minds and see our intentions come to fruition in our lives. We covered meditation in a previous chapter (and we'll revisit it later), and we'll look at how to set up your daily practice in the next chapter, but right now I want to introduce you to the concept of ritual.

Ritual

Ritual is a good descriptive word for many spiritual practices, on both the personal and community levels. Lots of people dislike the very idea of ritual—which suggests to me that they have a lot of negative experiences around it, usually related to the church of their childhood, and don't understand the depth and extent of ritual experience. Some people call ritual "ceremony" because that word doesn't have as much baggage attached. Others insist that ritual and ceremony are different things (though there's no agreement on the differences).

Ritual often is defined as a series of actions regularly repeated in a particular order—and yeah, that can get pretty boring and uninspiring. Some of the many objections to rituals that I've heard are that rituals use symbols participants don't understand or espouse beliefs they don't hold and that rituals are at best boring and can even be actively harmful in some instances.

But ritual is what you make of it, and it can be not only transformative but mad fun as well. Done with intention, creativity, and understanding, ritual anchors our intentions in the physical world and infuses the pattern we create with the power of spirit. This kind of thoughtful ritual shifts and changes our brains and personal energy field as well as the energy of the space it's conducted in. It helps us connect with others and create a tapestry of mutual intent. It lets us interact with the world of spirit by creating an energetic, psychic, and physical container for that interaction. Many ritualists refer to that container as "sacred space." Intentional ritual is one of the most valuable tools in your spiritual toolbox because good ritual affects us on all levels—physical, mental, emotional, and spiritual.

Ritual doesn't have to be rigid and dictated from on high, following a carefully written script. In fact, many people's objection to ritual is that it is "scripted." It depends on the script, but I agree that institutionalized ritual often ranges from deadly dull to risible. When it's done well, ritual can be moving and transformative, particularly if you subscribe to the beliefs that underlie the observance. Done poorly, you could be put off ritual for life. (Which would be a shame!) I've been in plenty of rituals that were so bad I had trouble keeping a straight face, but there have been many more that inspired and changed me in ways that simple prayer or meditation never did.

I've found that people with theatrical training often make excellent ritualists because they have learned to choose good scripts and stage them well. (People don't object to Broadway plays because they're "scripted.") Ritual, like a good play, takes us to a different level of consciousness. It can be as planned as carefully as a Broadway production or be spontaneous and improvised in the moment. Unlike a play, the best rituals demand the participation of everyone there. There is no audience. Rituals should be enjoyable—done well, they are transformative, and it's hard to transform when one is bored or resisting. Even at its most serious, ritual should be compelling and engaging.

Of course, there are rituals that are designed to *not* transform you, to keep you in line, doing the what the ritual organizers want you to do. Most of us participate in rituals that we may not even realize are rituals, from the eager brainwashing of a corporate national sales meeting to a political rally to various sports events, protests, and marches. Needless to say, religious rituals often fall under this umbrella of rituals designed to keep people in line with both prescribed and proscribed behavior and rigid dogma. But conscious, intentional ritual, designed to engage us on all levels of mind, body, and spirit, is how we can discover and change unconscious patterns that are running our lives.

You can do ritual by yourself or you can do it with others. You can plan it carefully or make it up as you go. But do give it a try. (If you did the purification bath in chapter 6, you already have!) Read a couple of books and make a point of going to a few public rituals as an observer. Most religions offer rituals that are open to the public, and your nearest metaphysical bookstore will probably have or know about local drum circles, perhaps a class on ritual, and maybe New Moon circles or Pagan Sabbat celebrations that are open to the public. When you attend these rituals, go with an inquiring, observing mind, but also with a respectful attitude and an open heart. You may find that even though the underlying philosophy is not yours and the symbol set is a strange one, you leave the ritual changed for the better. I hope you'll read at least one or two of the books on ritual at the end of this chapter and give the ideas in them a try.

Altars

One important (though not essential) component of ritual is the altar, a sort of control center for the ritual where the spirit and the physical meet to create a space between the two worlds. Since we are here in the reality of time and space, it's useful to have a place in our homes that will hold the energy of spirit and help keep us in touch with our spiritual allies and personal goals. It's also a place to keep magical tools and other physical items that you may be working with in your practice. Eventually, the altar itself becomes a portal between the worlds.

I have to admit that I have about nine or ten altars in my small house, with my primary altar—a low, round table—in my bedroom along with several other altars on shelves that are dedicated to some aspect of my life—business and finance, relationships (including relationships with the land spirits where I live)—and to my ancestors and guiding deities.

You don't need to get that elaborate, but it would be helpful to have a small area—even just a square foot of bookshelf or dresser space—dedicated to your spiritual inquiries. If you're not sure what to put on it, start with one thing for each of the four classical elements (more on that in chapter 13). Here are some ideas:

- Air: A feather, incense, a gong, a bell, tingshas, or a rattle.
- Water: A bowl or cup of some kind, preferably with water in it. Seashells work too.
- Earth: A stone or crystal, or a small dish of salt.
- Fire: A candle is ideal—preferably red—but you could also use a symbol or picture of the Sun or a fire.

For fire, some people like electric candles. I don't—it's just more plastic crap eventually destined for the landfill, and to my mind and senses, it does not have the same transformative, cleansing energy as live fire. If you must go electric, then at least get a "candle" that is made to last and allows you to change the bulb and battery instead of throwing the whole thing out.

You can also put any objects you own that you feel are sacred, including ancestral tokens or simply some natural object you picked up that serves to remind you of your connection with Nature or spirit. As you continue your spiritual journey, your altar(s) will change as you do. For instance, if you start working with specific deities or spirits, you might incorporate objects on your altar that serve as something like a "seat" for them—an object that helps them connect with you and your physical life. (We'll get into that more in chapter 11.) If you absolutely can't find space for an altar in your home, you can also keep an altar in a box that you bring out and open when you are meditating or working magic.

For now, just follow your instinct about what to put on your altar, and/or read one or two of the books listed below. Just make sure you treat it and everything on your altar with respect, which means tending it regularly—dusting, changing the water, lighting the candle, etc.

Once you have your altar set up, you might want to give creating sacred space a try. This involves working with subtle energies, so let's look at what they are.

Energy

Merriam-Webster offers this definition of energy: "a fundamental entity of nature that is transferred between parts of a system in the production of physical change within the system and usually regarded as the capacity for doing work."

Humans have defined and measured many forms of energy—kinetic, electrical, chemical, etc. Another form of energy—defining energy as "an entity that produces physical change"—that we have not been able to measure is the basis of a number of methodologies, including acupuncture, hands-on healing, magic, sacred geometry, ley lines, etc. It is called chi, prana, mana, life energy, orgone, and many other names by practitioners of those modalities. (While there are differences in these subtle energies, just as there are differences between kinetic, electrical, and chemical energy, for the sake of the argument I'm going to lump the energies we can't yet measure together as "subtle" energy.)

That we cannot define or measure subtle energy does not, of course, mean that it doesn't exist. Our abilities to scientifically measure various types of energy are only a few hundred years old, but the energies themselves have been around since the dawn of time. I believe these subtle energies are the bridge between pure Consciousness and material creation within time and space.

If we can't define or measure the energies themselves, then we must see if we can manipulate them and measure their effects. The modalities above that are based on these energies have given us some remarkably detailed maps, but for the moment, the only measuring device for these energies are the human mind and body. We see it used in acupuncture, the martial arts, and various healing practices. Yoga and acupuncture texts map out pathways of energy that show marked differences between the systems but remarkable likenesses as well, just as you might expect from, say, a map of the nervous system compared with a map of the circulatory system.

It's useful when trying to conceptualize these energies to consider how electrical energy is generated and distributed. Electrical energy is created in a generating station, which sends it out at a very high voltage along those giant electrical transmission lines that stretch across the land. It is gathered for local distribution at substations, where devices called step-down transformers take the high-voltage energy and reduce it to a lower voltage before sending it out along lines that carry it to the consumer. Its voltage is reduced again by another step-down transformer before entering our buildings.

The subtle energies, to my mind, are step-down transformers for reality creation. This is how the intense, high-voltage, pure awareness of Consciousness creates within in our world of time and space. This is how thoughts become things, how Consciousness creates the physical realm, by moderating and modulating itself to be distributed through our realm in a form that we can use to create within our limited world.

We may not have a machine to measure this energy, but we have our bodies and brains. Once you start this work, you'll eventually be able to sense some subtle energies yourself. You'll learn to perceive stuck energy patterns and release them, to gather energy and distribute it. It may be healing energy, or a punch that carries chi along with the kinetic energy. Like fire, these energies can be used to heal or to harm. But learning to sense and control them is the first step.

There are a number of ways we can work with this energy to increase our awareness of it and to deepen and strengthen our connection to the world of spirit. One of the best ways to begin to increase your awareness is to create sacred space in your home. I'll give you a simple way to do that in the next chapter but do read some of the books listed below if you want to make your home into a place of both refuge and transformation.

Now that you have an altar and a understanding of energy and ritual, let's look at creating a daily practice and seasonal ritual in the next chapter.

Resources

Ritual

Murry Hope, *The Psychology of Ritual* (Rockport: Element Books Ltd, 1991).

Malidoma Patrice Somé, *Ritual: Power, Healing, and Community* (London: Penguin Books, 1997).

Azrael Arynn K and Amber K, *RitualCraft: Creating Rites for Transformation and Celebration* (St. Paul: Llewellyn Publications, 2006).

Renee Beck and Sydney Barbara Metrick, *The Art of Ritual: Creating and Performing Ceremonies for Growth and Change* (Berkeley: Apocryphile Press, 2009).

Deborah Lipp, *The Elements of Ritual: Air, Fire, Water & Earth in the Wiccan Circle* (St. Paul: Llewellyn Publications, 2003).

Jane Meredith, *Rituals of Celebration: Honoring the Seasons of Life through the Wheel of the Year* (St. Paul: Llewellyn Publications, 2013).

Nadine Epstein and Rosita Arvigo, *Spiritual Bathing: Healing Rituals and Traditions from Around the World* (Brattleboro: Echo Point Books & Media, 2018).

Altars and Sacred Space

Ivo Dominguez, Jr., *Casting Sacred Space: The Core of All Magickal Work* (Newburyport: Weiser Books, 2012).

Denise Linn, *Altars: Bringing Sacred Shrines into Your Everyday Life* (New York: Wellspring/Ballantine, 1999).

Denise Linn, *Sacred Space: Clearing and Enhancing the Energy of Your Home* (New York: Wellspring/Ballantine, 2007).

Jagatjoti Singh Khalsa, *Altar Your Space: A Guide to the Restorative Home* (San Rafael: Mandala Publishing, 2007).

Sandra Kynes, *Your Altar: Creating a Sacred Space for Prayer & Meditation* (St. Paul: Llewellyn Publications, 2007).

Energy

Anodea Judith, *Charge and the Energy Body: The Vital Key to Healing Your Life, Your Chakras, and Your Relationships* (Carlsbad: Hay House, 2018).

David Spangler, *Working With Subtle Energies* (Traverse City: Lorian Press, 2016).

Deborah Lipp, *Magical Power For Beginners: How to Raise & Send Energy for Spells That Work* (St. Paul: Llewellyn Publications, 2017).

Cyndi Dale, *Subtle Energy Techniques* (St. Paul: Llewellyn Publications, 2017).

Penney Peirce, *Frequency: The Power of Personal Vibration* (New York: Atria Books, 2009).

Wilhelm Reich, *Selected Writings: An Introduction to Orgonomy* (New York: Farrar, Straus and Giroux, 2013).

Richard Gerber, *Vibrational Medicine* (Rochester: Bear & Company, 2001).

CHAPTER EIGHT
Ostara—The Spring Equinox

As the Sun waxes and the weather warms moving into spring, we'll look at how we can connect our spiritual path to our everyday life. The Spring Equinox—a.k.a. Ostara, Lady Day, Alban Eilir—is a time when day and night are of equal length, buds are swelling on trees, and seeds are stirring in the ground. It's a time to plant—magically as well as physically. Nature has its own magic, and you can draw on it to enhance your personal magical intentions and rituals. How do you do this? Let's first consider what Nature is—the planet and the life that it engendered.

Earth—the planet itself—is not inert. It has an inner core of mostly iron that is the same temperature as the Sun's surface, and a fiery, liquid outer core of nickel and iron. Above that is the rocky mantle, and finally, the crust, the surface of the planet.

Our planet also is graced with rivers and oceans and an atmosphere with its accompanying winds and storms. You can find most of these things—or traces of them—on other planets in our solar system. But somehow, what we call life sprang into being on this planet and no other. We have some idea of how this may have happened—primordial soup, single cells to multi-cellular beings, crawling out of the ocean up on the land. Structures developing—fin, leaf, bone, root, fur, and feather, etc. The slow, inevitable, creative process of evolution. If Consciousness is the ground of all reality, then life must be one of its most complex creative endeavors.

Now, keep in mind that this is not an argument for so-called "intelligent design," which postulates an external creator ("God") that directs natural processes in line with its (usually referred to as "His") desired outcome. Consciousness is not external to what it creates. It is inherent in every atom and cell, in the natural processes of evolution. It connects us all in a web of life, death, and rebirth.

We sense this connection when we stand in awe of a sunrise, hug a child, walk in the woods, help a friend, or fall in love. We feel it also when we face a friend's death, see a child cry, view the trashed remains of trees on a clear-cut hillside, or realize we have inadvertently hurt someone we love. But whether we sense it or not, that connection is always there. Learning how we can make the most of our lives on this amazing planet, how we can develop our own powers of creation to shift and change the world around us, is the work of science and also of magic.

Becoming more sensitive to the subtle energies I discussed in the last chapter is an important step in spiritual and magical development because it not only enhances awareness of that connection but allows us to draw on the energies of the natural world to strengthen and propel our magic into manifestation.

Recall that energy is defined as "the ability to do work." The original work of this world is the work that brings Consciousness into manifestation. This happens in a liminal space that we are only beginning to understand scientifically but we are still connected to through every atom of our being. Learning to use that connection with insight and skill allows us to influence what manifests in our lives. We call that influence magic.

It may seem utterly impossible that anointing a candle of a specific color with an oil made from certain herbs and burning it can have any effect on whether or not you get a job or a new lover or sell your house. But recall the discussion of subtle energies and resonance. What these spells are doing is increasing the resonance of the desired outcome in your mind, in your aura, and so in the world around you. The herbs, the candle, the flame, and your mind all come into the resonant frequency of that subtle energy of manifestation. Whether or not you hit the exact right frequency that shatters the glass, that shifts and changes other frequencies that may be working against your outcome, depends, to a great extent, on your skill as a magician. So let's look at the next steps you can take in developing that skill during this time when the burgeoning energy of life is so close to the surface, so easy to sense and access.

⊣ TOUCH THE EARTH ⊢

Setting Up an Altar

Set up an altar. Ideally, you've read one or two of the books mentioned in the last chapter, but you don't need to get fancy here. Just find a place that can be a physical focus for your spiritual work and put some things on it that are meaningful to you. I like to change the items on my altar with each Sabbat—the color of the cloth and candles, the bowl, candle holders and other accoutrements, and some seasonal plant—flowers, leaves, fruits, and in winter, bare branches painted white scattered with a bit of biodegradable (not plastic!) silver glitter. (If you're harvesting from a living plant, do so with care and consideration for the plant and the local ecology.) Set your altar up in any way that works for you with your own personal symbolism.

Sensing Subtle Energy

Practice sensing subtle energy. Many of the books in the resources section of the last chapter have training exercises (and there are more in the next chapter about human energy fields specifically), but here's a simple one to get you started:

- Sit comfortably, take a few deep breaths, and settle your mind into the present moment.
- Rub your hands together briskly for fifteen to thirty seconds.
- Hold your hands in front of you, elbows bent, palms facing each other.
- Bring your hands as close together as you can without touching, paying close attention to any sensations in your hands. Don't worry about whether or not you are "imagining" it. Just allow yourself to feel.
- Going very slowly, separate your hands about a foot apart. Pay attention to the sensations in your palms.
- Repeat several times.

If you don't feel anything at first, keep trying. Do a little bit every day. Eventually, you'll sense the energy, probably as heat, or tingling, or pressure in your palms. See if you can eventually form a ball of energy that you can sense. When you're finished with your practice, move the ball of energy in front of your heart and fill it with as much love and/or other positive emotion as you can muster. Then fling both hands outward and release it to the universe.

You can also practice by trying to sense the energy of a space. Any space has its own energy which is affected by a number of factors—geography, construction materials, history and hauntings, and the people in or very near it, to name just a few. I expect that most of you understand what I'm conveying here because you've experienced it. A helpful exercise is to take the time to explore and invite those experiences. Here are some ideas (practice them both at home and away from home):

- Pause before a closed door. Come into the present moment. Sense any thoughts or emotions that come up as you face the door. Imagine your awareness extending past the door. What do you sense about the energy of the people and the space on the other side of the door?

- Do this again once you have walked through the door and are actually in the space.

- Go out into Nature (even if it's just a small city park) and sit quietly, allowing your awareness to be fully in the present moment. Can you sense the energy of individual trees, plants, animals? How is the energy of this space different from your home, from your office, from a store in a shopping mall?

- Do some things to change the energy of a space you have some control over. If you have roommates, office mates, or family that will play along with you, even better. Physically cleaning, lighting candles, doing meditation in the space, singing or chanting, burning incense—try some or all of these techniques, and note the changes you sense. I especially recommend the books on space clearing in chapter 6.

The key here is not to get discouraged. In the same way that you have to develop an ear for different instruments and arrangements in music, an eye for composition and brushstroke in painting, a palate that can distinguish the subtle flavors of wine or whiskey, so your psychic senses will develop slowly and with experience.

Experiencing Ritual

Attend some rituals. They can be church services, Pagan circles, or even political rallies or sports events. Not all rituals are spiritually oriented, but they all shift energy.

If possible, get there a little early so you can get a sense of the space before a lot of people get there. Try to tune in, to sense the resonance of the space as the participants arrive and take their places. Note how the energy changes as the ritual progresses, how it is affected by the people who are participating, and how it affects them—including yourself, of course. (Don't think you can be a detached observer. Just by being there, you affect the energy of the ritual.)

Sense how the energy of the ritual winds down, and note if it is actively shut down, as it generally will be in a Pagan circle. Usually, it simply dissipates as people leave. If possible, talk to some of the participants afterward and ask them how they felt their own mood or energy change during the ritual.

When you get home, write in your journal about your experiences. In this kind of work it's important to trust your instincts. Don't worry about whether or not you got it "right." Just write down what you sensed or think you sensed. It can be helpful to have a friend or a group of friends who share your interest in this work go to these rituals with you so you can compare notes.

Spellwork

Now it's time to try an actual spell! Find a way to grow a plant from seed over the summer. A pot on a sunny balcony or window is fine. If you have no way of putting a pot in sunlight, a plant light is OK too. Marigolds or basil are both good choices—especially basil if you can only grow indoors in a window or under a light. Do a bit of research on how to properly plant the seeds and grow whatever plant you choose and go shopping for whatever supplies you need—seeds, pot, soil, etc.

Decide on something you want to grow and expand in your life, something you are ready to put some energy into, something that you plan to take action to create. Prepare the pot with soil and a saucer. Wet the soil in the pot in advance of the ritual and give it an hour or so to drain. You'll be adding a bit more water during the spell.

Prepare your altar with a candle, some incense, and a small pitcher of water (you won't need much since you already dampened the soil). Dump the seeds out of the packet into a small bowl or saucer. You'll also need a small piece of paper (around 3 inches x 3 inches), a pen, and a small stick, like a popsicle stick or skewer. The pot with the dampened soil should also be on the altar with the saucer underneath it.

Light a candle and perhaps some incense to help you ground and center. Settle in. Bring yourself fully into the present moment and let your worries and cares drop away.

Think about the thing you want to grow and how it will change your life. Flesh out this dream in your mind. How does your daily life change in this dream? How will it feel when you wake up in the morning and the dream has come true? Don't think about the "how." Yes, you'll need to plan and take specific actions, but planning is for another time. Now you just want to focus on the results you want and how you will feel when you've achieved them.

Write or draw what you want on the piece of paper—just a sentence or two, or a symbol, not a detailed report. Fold the paper toward you, then turn it 90 degrees and fold it again. Do that one more time if possible. Bury it in the pot, using the stick to poke it down into the soil, then level out the soil over it.

Next, take the bowl of seeds and hold it between your hands for a minute as you open yourself to sensing the life energy contained within the seeds. (Don't get all in your head about this. Just see what thoughts and feelings arise as you focus on the seeds.) Then, carefully and with your full attention, pick one seed. Just one.

Put the seed in the palm of one hand and cover it with the other. Spend a few minutes imbuing the seed with the energy of your dream, of your goal. Focus on your dream and let the energy flow from your gut, your heart, and your head through your hands into the seed. When it feels like you've done that long enough (trust your instincts!), plant the seed carefully at the appropriate depth (check the seed packet) and press the soil down.

Then take the pitcher of water, hold it between your hands, and bless it with the energy of your dream. Water the seed in with some of the blessed water (not too much!) and put it where it can grow. Once it germinates and begins to grow, you'll need to either pot it up into larger pots or plant it outdoors. Make sure all the soil goes with it!

This little spell serves to magically energize your goal, but also gives you a way of assessing what's going on.

Does the seed fail to germinate? Ask yourself what's needed to energize your goal or if you have enough knowledge about how to achieve your dream. Also consider if this is something you really want. Sometimes we think we want something that is really what others in our lives want for us. Is your desire coming from your own soul or are you trying to fulfill your parents' or spouse's expectations of you? I said to pick only one seed for this reason. Whether or not that single seed germinates gives you clear guidance as to whether you're on to something or need to do more foundational work and research.

Does the seed germinate but the little plant dies soon after? Ask yourself what resources your goal needs that you may not have planned for.

Does the plant grow well but not flower? Perhaps the timing is right for working on your goal but not right for your plans to come to fruition. Or you may need more input of some kind for your plans to bear fruit. You can look for more insight into the issues involved through meditation and divination. If you aren't experienced with divination (or even if you are but feel too emotionally attached to the issue to be objective), then get a reading from a reputable professional. Ask friends or check with your local metaphysical store for recommendations. These days, a lot of good diviners work online.

If the plant survives and flowers, chances are good that your plans are moving ahead. Each time you care for the plant as it grows, you are adding magical energy to your goal. Once the plant flowers, let the flowers go to seed. Collect the seed and use them in magical talismans (more on those later in the book) and/or save some to plant next year.

Daily Work

Finally, start some kind of daily spiritual practice over these next six weeks. Let's consider what that might look like in the Kiss the Sky section.

─┤ KISS THE SKY ├─

Spiritual Practice

Spring is a good time to review your daily habits and think about how you want to change them. If you can do this while you are outside in Nature, so much the better! Then when you get back home, pull out your journal and put your ideas and resolutions on paper. You'll be much more likely to follow up if you do that.

What should your daily practice be? I'd suggest reading one or two of the books I recommend at the end of this chapter, but at the least, I'd suggest a few minutes of meditation, grounding and centering, and some time spent tuning in to and improving the health of your physical body.

Don't beat yourself up over missing a day, a few days, or even an extended period of time. Self-shaming and blaming are self-destructive and entirely counter-productive to the intent of a daily spiritual practice. I used to do that a lot, so I speak from experience. I have an agile and restless mind that demands variety. I dislike doing the same thing at the same time of day every day. And yet even I recognize the value of repetition, of scheduling, and of some kind of daily spiritual work or play.

I noticed I did always manage to have my morning cup of coffee, usually first thing, but not always. So I started to explore my resistance to daily practice by watching what I enjoyed doing. Coffee-making was invariably accompanied by some of the usual little household rituals—emptying the dishwasher, opening blinds, etc. Hmmm … this is repetitive, but I don't resist it, I thought. So I began to tie my daily writing practice to drinking my coffee. I'd take the sacred beverage back to bed with my laptop and write pretty much every morning. That's why you're reading this book. Yes, sometimes I read instead. That's OK. Meditation and Yoga follow coffee—most of the time. Some days, if I get up earlier, I meditate, work a bit of magic at my altar, and/or do Yoga first.

If I don't get things done in the morning, I try to fit them in later. But I do manage to meditate, exercise, and write at least four or five days a week, and

I consider that enough, if not ideal. I used to admonish myself for skipped days. No longer. Skipped days are just part of my process and the cycles of my life. Now I tend to simply fit things in when and where I can, not berating myself or worrying if I don't do everything exactly right, particularly if things are going along reasonably well in my life and I don't see any clouds on the horizon astrologically.

Yes, self-discipline is necessary, but we should not become rigid. We need to learn to listen to our souls. Often, on those days when I don't do what I "should" do, I end up doing something else that I only realize later was what I really needed—perhaps an extra hour of sleep, or reading another chapter in a book that gave me the inspiration I needed to make the day go right.

I suggest approaching a daily practice as a work in progress. Find what works for you, and then keep adjusting it as needed. Pay attention to your desires and urges to do or not do something. Where do they originate? Eventually, it will become easier to differentiate between messages from your soul and habitual self-indulgent or self-punishing behaviors that are sourced in negative beliefs and ideas.

Finding the Four Directions

At Spring Equinox, Sun rises directly in the east. What marks that spot where you live? On the day of the equinox, stand facing east and stretch your arms directly out to your sides. Your right hand is pointing south. Your left hand is pointing north. West is directly behind you.

The equal-armed cross is an ancient symbol of manifestation. Consider, as you stand at the center of the cross of the four cardinal directions, that you stand in a magical place, a place of creation, a place of magical power. We'll be working with the four cardinal directions later in the book. For now, spend some time orienting yourself as you go through your day. Where is Sun in the sky? What direction are you moving in? Practicing magic in concert with Nature requires both knowledge and experience of your immediate environment. This practice will help get you oriented and prepare you for working with the elements through the four directions.

Learning Your Local Ecology

Spend some time thinking and learning about the complex interactions that create and sustain life on this planet. This may involve trips to the library to check out some books on subjects like geology, ecology, weather, marine life, or botany. As you study, keep in mind the phrase "think globally, act locally." You'll want to have a broad understanding of global ecology and how changes in one area of the planet affects other areas. That knowledge can strengthen your magic. But the strongest magic of Nature that is available to you is local, so be sure to spend some time learning about your local geology and ecology.

As you explore Nature, it's important to remember that Nature is not just outside of you. You are part of Nature too, and your body is a powerful magical tool. Let's look at that next.

Resources

Kerri Connor, *Ostara: Rituals, Recipes & Lore for the Spring Equinox* (St. Paul: Llewellyn Publications, 2015).

Ellen Dugan, *Garden Witchery: Magick from the Ground Up* (St. Paul: Llewellyn Publications, 2013).

Rupert Sheldrake, *Science and Spiritual Practices: Transformative Experiences and Their Effects on Our Bodies, Brains, and Health* (Berkeley: Counterpoint Press, 2018).

Caroline Myss, Ph.D., *Spiritual Power, Spiritual Practice: Energy Evaluation Meditations for Morning and Evening* Audiobook (Boulder: Sounds True, 1999).

Gabrielle Roth, *Sweat Your Prayers: The Five Rhythms of the Soul—Movement as Spiritual Practice* (New York: Tarcher, 2002).

Tom Cowan, *Shamanism as a Spiritual Practice for Daily Life* (Berkeley: Crossing Press, 2014).

Timothy Roderick, *Wicca: A Year and a Day: 366 Days of Spiritual Practice in the Craft of the Wise* (St. Paul: Llewellyn Publications, 2013).

Ernest Callenbach, *Ecology: A Pocket Guide* (Oakland: University of California Press, 2008).

Llewellyn Vaughan-Lee, *Spiritual Ecology: 10 Practices to Reawaken the Sacred in Everyday Life* (Point Reyes Station: Golden Sufi Center, 2017).

Ellen Moyer, *Our Earth, Our Species, Our Selves: How to Thrive While Creating a Sustainable World* (Montgomery: Greenvironment Press, 2016).

Wendell Berry, *The Unsettling of America: Culture & Agriculture* (Berkeley: Counterpoint Press, 2015).

The Cooperative Extension Service, a subset of the US Department of Agriculture, is a tremendous resource for education about agriculture and natural resources. Go to https://nifa.usda.gov/extension to find your local extension service.

The Temple of the Soul

Our soul, spirit, Greater Self—whatever name you prefer for that larger awareness we are part of that is eternal—can only become fully manifest in this time-and-space world through a body. In life, it connects us to physical existence; in death, our body is the only part of us that we leave in the physical realm, to decay back into the stuff of Earth and be reborn once again as another form of life through Nature's extraordinary magic.

Unfortunately, all too often we find ourselves in an adversarial relationship with our bodies, which are rather fragile and prone to pain, illness, and aging. The question of how much control we have over them—over our health—is an ongoing one. Currently, it appears that at least some of us have the ability—sometimes, in some situations—to heal ourselves and others through various nonphysical means—magical intention and laying on of hands, for example. It's been repeatedly shown in multiple peer-reviewed scientific experiments that our thoughts can and do affect aspects of our health, such as blood pressure and certain aspects of our biochemistry. None of this means we can "think away" cancer or any other illness. It does mean that with further evolution, exploration, and training, we may be able to use our minds even more effectively to improve our health.

If our birth onto this plane of existence was a conscious, willing choice, then we knew what we were getting into—this crazy, convoluted, polluted, and unhealthy culture we have created that is nonetheless one of the most remarkable and creative in our history—and so we knew what was possible.

We knew what might happen. We knew we might get cancer or arthritis or lose our legs in war. We also may have chosen to be born into a body that is challenged by genetics and/or the environment we were born into.

It's hard for us to wrap our minds around why anyone would choose to be born, for instance, with no arms or legs, or blind and deaf. But that's our ego sitting in the CEO's office again. We simply can't fully understand the choices made by our Greater Self; we can only assume that their reasons are creative and proceed with our lives, taking full advantage of the options we do have. (And if you think those options must necessarily be poor ones, Helen Keller or Nick Vujicic might change your mind.) We simply cannot know what questions another person's soul is asking. We have a hard-enough time figuring out our own.

To experience this life in physical reality in a way that is fully engaged and creative, we can't come into this world with full awareness of our previous lives and the entirety of our Greater Self. The narrow awareness we take on when we are embodied is deliberate and creative. Even when life gets unbearably difficult, to create freely we must assume we are not enslaved to some deity who is testing us to see if we're good enough to get to some better place. We are autonomous beings who have chosen to take on this challenge of physical reality, and we can do that only through the amazing creation that is our body.

Our body invariably reflects our soul's concerns, both through our genes and our current health. No, this is not victim-blaming. People who have serious medical problems did not consciously choose to be ill or disabled, and relative health or illness does not reflect spiritual progress or the lack of it. But on some level, we all chose to be born. Our Greater Self chose—or at least acquiesced to—our genetic makeup, our parents, and the environment into which we were born.

A firefighter, a police officer, a mercenary soldier, a health care professional choosing to work in an area scourged by infectious disease, a jockey, a race car driver, they all regularly put themselves in situations where their bodies—indeed, their very lives—are at extreme risk. Is it so hard to consider that we might all have been willing to do something similar just by agreeing to be born?

We forget all that after we get here—usually in the preverbal stage, maybe even in the womb. We even forget why we chose as we did and find ourselves enmeshed in a world where we affect and are affected by each other and the environment every single day. The choices we make, as well as the choices others make that affect us, have a huge influence on our health and well-being. It's all part of the challenge, part of our studies and explorations in becoming a conscious creator within this dimension of reality.

As students of creation, we explore different areas of experience—thought, will, emotion, and manifestation. We will come to comprehend the reasons behind our Greater Self's choices eventually, but railing against them, or against what is in the past, gets us nowhere. What gets us somewhere is making choices and taking advantage of opportunities with as much wisdom and insight as we can muster. We develop these qualities by learning how our minds work, improving self-discipline, refining awareness, having the courage to face what we fear. Our bodies will help us do these things if we learn to pay attention.

The Subtle Bodies

Your body is a magical tool. It is the interface your soul has created to manifest within physical reality. Learning to listen to your body is a necessary step on any healthy, progressive spiritual path.

If subtle energies are the bridge between Consciousness and creation, then it makes sense that our bodies would have energetic "blueprints" that mediate the layered shift from Consciousness into physicality. Indeed, the healing modalities of many non-Western cultures involve working with subtle energy on one level or another. Acupuncture, Ayurveda, Reiki, and traditional Chinese medicine (TCM) all focus on shifting the energetic vibration of the subtle bodies.

What are the subtle bodies? Because we cannot yet measure subtle energies, we must rely on the effects we can measure and the visionary abilities of great healers to determine and define what these bodies are and how we can work with them toward our own healing.

Those effects are there, and they are real. The composition and structures of various energy bodies is a hotly debated subject, and I am not going to join that debate here. Refer to the resources section at the end of this chapter if you want to dive into the topic. For now, I'll just describe the concepts that I have found most useful and work with myself. You'll find that most of them are from the Yogic tradition because that's what I began studying intensively in my teens and have been working with ever since. Some are from Chinese traditions of energy work because I studied Chinese martial arts for many years. There are certainly other traditions of energetic healing, and I encourage you to explore them, but here are some insights I've gleaned over the years.

I've found that the energy centers and pathways of both Yoga and TCM are valid and useful. People have asked me over the years how they can both be "right." These different systems of energy are like the nervous system, the circulatory system, and the skeleton. They all exist, they are all part of the body, but if you look at them all separately, they don't look at all alike.

These two maps of the energy body even seem to overlap—the three *dan tiens* (lower, middle, and upper) of TCM occupy more or less the same locations as three of the *chakras* of Yoga, and both traditions recognize the spine as a primary transmitter of energy. But I am not convinced that the second chakra and the lower dan tien, for instance, are the same thing. Same general location, but my sense of each is different. Further thought led me to consider whether or not we might all have all of these energy centers but pattern and imprint our energy bodies in line with the tradition we are working in. The parts of our brains that perceive subtle energies may be tuned to different frequencies and patterns of energy. With practice, it seems we can widen our perceptions to include new frequencies and patterns.

I'm still pondering this question of how the different systems are related. In the meantime, I keep practicing Yoga and Tai Chi, meditating, and working on fully occupying my body using the following patterns for insight and awareness.

The Chakras

The chakras are primarily from the Hindu/Yogic tradition, though other cultures locate similar energetic structures in similar locations. There are quite a few, but seven main ones along the spinal column are the ones usually shown. Many people (myself included) work with a transpersonal chakra about a foot above the head, which I see ranging between white/silver/rainbow. I also work with a chakra about a foot below me in the earth, which ranges from gold to red. I know of a few others who work with that one. There's an even deeper one than that, but I don't work with it. I just sense it sometimes as part of my connection to Earth.

In addition to the chakras, the *nadis* are important channels of energy in Yoga. There are tens of thousands of them, but the primary ones are the *sushumna*, the "great river" that runs from the base of the spine to the crown of the head, and the two ancillary ones that twist around it, like the snakes on the caduceus—the *ida* (beginning and ending on the left) and the *pingala*, (beginning and ending on the right). One important breathing exercise (*pranayama*) in Yoga, alternate-nostril breathing, is designed to balance *prana* (energy) on its journey through these nadis.

Yoga is designed to direct, strengthen, and moderate (as necessary) the flow of prana throughout the body. It also helps us become more aware of our energy bodies. Practicing Yoga is an excellent way to strengthen your energy bodies as well as your physical body.

Learning to visualize and work with the chakras is a relatively easy and powerful way of meditating on your own healing and learning to sense subtle energy. Beginning a Yoga practice, particularly one that includes pranayama and learning to visualize the chakras is a great way to expand your awareness of this invisible world of energy and improve your health at the same time. Yoga can be done by anyone who can move—even slightly—and breathe. It is all about focusing your mind on your body and doing whatever you can in the moment, even if that's only rotating your ankles or turning your head from one side to the other.

The Meridians

Meridians are paths of energy through which *chi* ("energy," also spelled *qi*) flows in the body and are the energy pathways defined and used by TCM. Acupuncture uses certain points along these meridians to redirect, strengthen, or moderate the flow of chi through these channels. (Chinese martial arts use many of those same points to disable or even kill an opponent.) While I occasionally use acupuncture points or pathways myself (for instance, massaging the point between thumb and first finger when I get a headache), I usually leave any manipulation of these points to my acupuncturist and massage therapist. My level of knowledge about TCM is fairly broad but not very deep.

TCM also postulates three energy centers—the three dan tiens—that are roughly in line with three of the chakras, but are not, I believe, the same thing. The lower dan tien is at the location of the second chakra, the middle dan tien is roughly at the location of the fourth chakra, and the upper dan tien is at the location of the sixth chakra, shading into the seventh. The differences will become more obvious to you as you investigate both, but to put it simply, my understanding is that chakras are vortices that deal with the flow of subtle energy and how it connects us with this world and larger realities, while the dan tiens deal more with subtle energy storage and distribution within the body.

Tai Chi and Qigong are designed to enhance and strengthen the flow of chi through the body, so learning either of these disciplines will improve your health, your mental concentration, and help you become more aware of your energy bodies. Qigong is the gentler of the two practices and focuses primarily on the movement of subtle energy. Though Tai Chi is a practice of slow and deliberate motion, it is a martial art, and if you get into the advanced stages, you will learn to utilize energy in self-defense.

I do not recommend starting both a Yoga practice and a Tai Chi practice at the same time, but once you have worked with one for a while, you might want to try the other, and you may find that you want to fit both into your personal practice.

The Aura and the Subtle Bodies

The concept of multiple layers of colored etheric energy surrounding the human body is widespread in cultures and religions. We find the concept in Hinduism, Yoga, Buddhism, Taoism, Chinese martial arts, the halos of Christian saints, and more modern interpretations, such as the work of Barbara Brennan and her ten-layered explication of the human auric field. I'm able to see simple, etheric auras, but mostly I just sense them in a more kinesthetic way. Some people seem to have a knack for seeing them, but don't get discouraged if you don't.

I believe these subtle bodies are the transformers, the blueprints that create a physical body from Consciousness. Those who can see them are tuning in to levels of reality that require perceptive abilities attuned to a vibrational level that is not apparent to our usual senses. I think actual changes need to happen in our brains to be able to perceive these levels.

In my experience, we can and do communicate with each other through these subtle bodies. Most of this communication is not conscious, but it probably accounts for a lot of "love at first sight," the sense we sometimes have of knowing someone we've just met, or how we cringe away from someone because they give off "bad vibes." We can learn to develop this ability and make it more conscious. I've found that to be a worthwhile effort, even though I expect I'll never "see" with the clarity and ability that many healers do. Of course, I'll never have a voice like Barbara Streisand's, either. But I can train and improve my own voice. Whether or not we have a lot of natural ability, we can work to train our sight to be more in tune with subtle energies.

Our Bodies, Our Selves

We only get one body and no maintenance manual. To my mind, one of the big spiritual questions is why the heck we crave certain foods, beverages, and drugs that do not support the health of our bodies, and why it can be so hard to shift our actions toward health. I suspect part of the answer has to do with physical evolution not keeping up with our creative mental evolution. Our big brains gave us ways to work around evolutionary needs, so we can now have as much sugar as we want, for instance, instead of craving the small amounts we could get from fruits and vegetables and the occasional honeycomb. It's beneficial to crave fruits and veggies, even sweet ones when calories are scarce. Craving ice cream, though, is not an evolutionary advantage, sadly.

Difficult though it may be, continuously working to improve/maintain health is an essential spiritual practice. The food we eat, the environment we experience, the exercise we get (or not), directly affects our mental state and our ability to pursue spiritual and material goals. Yet I frequently see people taking better care of their drums or crystals or tarot cards than they do of their own bodies.

Your body is your ultimate spiritual tool. No matter how many health challenges you are facing, no matter how adversarial your relationship with your body seems to be, it's important to learn to work with it, to do everything you can to support and maintain it. Yes, it is a temple. It's your temple, your soul's interface with the world, and it's the only one you've got.

Finding your way toward optimal health begins with paying attention to how you are feeling. Our culture as a whole does not have a healthy relationship with the body, and we are rarely taught to sense and tune in to our physical experience. This is one reason I recommend learning Yoga and/or Tai Chi and/or Qigong—these disciplines teach active awareness techniques for both the physical and subtle bodies. They have levels of practice that are accessible to almost anyone but scale up to levels that are quite demanding and strenuous for those who wish to take on that challenge.

But everyday awareness is important, too. Keep track of how various foods and activities affect you and tune in to your body when you are having an intense emotional experience. Learning the places where emotions manifest in your body can help you modulate your current emotions, release old, stored emotions from your past, and learn which areas of your body are weakened and need particular attention. Don't forget that simple grounding exercise I wrote about back in the chapter on Imbolc.

It is a rare person who can say they are eating and exercising optimally for the health of their body, so that is always a good place to begin your quest toward better health. Here are four things you can do right away:

1. You know that highly processed food isn't good for you. Learn to cook, if you don't know how already. Eat closer to the land.

2. Most of us eat way more sugar than our bodies evolved to deal with. Cut back. Way back.

3. Keep your alcohol consumption moderate and intermittent, not daily.

4. Exercise of some kind is of critical importance. Our bodies are meant to move. Even if your ability to move is limited, find the limits of what you are capable of, then do it.

5. Breathing. That seems obvious, doesn't it? But there are specific ways of working with the breath that have been codified through the centuries in Yoga and Tai Chi. In Yoga, breathing techniques are gathered under an umbrella of practice called pranayama. Pranayama is practiced on its own, but also integrated into the physical postures of Hatha Yoga

and different styles of meditation. In Tai Chi and Qigong, breathwork is generally integrated with the physical practice.

In both systems, the practice of breathing into your belly is important. This three-part breath is a good way to start a breathing practice. The resources section at the end of this chapter will help you discover more. Breathing consciously can have a big effect on your overall health. Here are instructions for the basic three-part breath to get you started.

Three-Part Breath

Take one of these poses: stand with your feet about hip distance apart, sit straight in a chair with feet on the floor, or sit on the floor in a comfortable, cross-legged position. Your spine should be straight, your shoulders back, and your chin up but not in a forced, military-like way. Move your spine around, roll your head and shoulders, rotate your hips, then find the position of your spine that feels naturally upright, giving maximum space to your lungs, freeing your diaphragm, and relieving any compression on your throat.

Exhale completely from the top of your lungs down to your belly. Squeeze out all the air. Then inhale into your belly alone, expanding it. Yes, your belly should stick out. If you're wearing something that won't accommodate that, then either loosen your clothing or change clothes. Once you have reached a full inhale into your belly, then exhale all the way, slowly contracting your belly to expel all the air. Repeat the belly breathing at least two or three times. There should be no pauses or held breath. Focus on a smooth inhale and exhale only in your belly area.

On your next inhale, after expanding your belly, continue inhaling into your middle chest area. Feel your back and ribs extend too. Now exhale fully, beginning in the middle chest, releasing the air downward until your belly contracts. Repeat at least two or three times.

When you are ready to continue, increase the inhale so it now comes all the way up into your upper chest. At this point, your belly may contract slightly, which is a natural adjustment, but focus on keeping it relaxed and open. Do not raise your shoulders. As soon as you reach maximum inhalation, immediately begin exhaling from your upper chest and let the exhale continue down until your lower belly contracts to expel all the air.

Once you have this third complete breath and are able to breath smoothly from your belly all the way up to the top of your chest, you can just do the three-part breath right from the beginning.

Practice this daily. Even just five or ten rounds will be helpful. Keep in mind, though, that this is an exercise, not a way you should try to breath regularly. But it would be good to work on training yourself to breath into your belly for your normal breathing. This is the way a baby breathes, and it is the best way to get oxygen in and toxins out of your lungs.

While you should always consult with your doctor about your diet and exercise routines, most doctors don't learn much about nutrition or optimal exercise in medical school. Their focus of learning is on illness, not health. So you'll want to do your own research and perhaps consult with a nutritionist and/or exercise coach. You might also want to consult with an Ayurvedic or TCM practitioner, since both of those healing modalities focus on using diet and exercise to improve health.

Mental Health

One of the reasons it's so hard for us to keep up with routines that we know are good for our health is that our thoughts and actions are, more often than not, driven by unconscious forces. Our physical health affects and is affected by our mental health. It's hard to stay mentally healthy in a society that is riddled with violence, suffering from the resulting trauma, and altering the environment in ways that are distinctly unhealthy.

Recognizing what is unhealthy in our society is a first step in healing our own mental illnesses, and few modern humans will not be touched by some level of depression, anxiety, PTSD, and/or some other form of mental illness at some point during our lives. Some of us will be so deeply affected—by anything from childhood trauma to our own genetic inheritance—that it can make us nonfunctional for periods of time or even permanently.

But the fact remains that no matter how disabled we are, physically or mentally, most of us have choices to make every day of our lives. We can choose to reach out for help. We can choose to practice shifting unhealthy patterns of thought. We can set intentions and choose to hold and nurture that intention. No one else can make those choices for us, even if they were willing and we asked. Sometimes those choices are hard and are driven by physical or mental needs or addictions. Sometimes we'll make the wrong choices. But it's important to recognize the choices we do have, to wrest those choices from the grasp of unconscious internal or negative external forces as best we can, and to ask for help when we can't.

If your mental health is having a negative impact on your life, get help. I've put some hotline information in the resources section, but the choice to call them is yours. The choice to find a therapist is yours. Admitting that you need help and accepting the help available is the first step to mental health, and there is no shame to this. But that first step to get and accept help is a decision only you can make.

Magic is work of the mind and the emotions. You can't just learn a few spells and then follow the steps by rote. That's not how it works. You have to put your focus, your energy, your magic into your spells. Your body and mind are your most important magical tools. Making sure they are in the best condition you can manage is an important first step on any spiritual journey.

Resources

Subtle Bodies and Energy Healing

Cyndi Dale, *The Subtle Body: An Encyclopedia of Your Energetic Anatomy* (Boulder: Sounds True, 2014).

Barbara Brennan, *Hands of Light: A Guide to Healing Through the Human Energy Field* (New York: Bantam Books, 1988).

Anodea Judith, *Wheels of Life: A User's Guide to the Chakra System* (St. Paul: Llewellyn Publications, 1987).

Richard Gerber, M.D., *A Practical Guide to Vibrational Medicine: Energy Healing and Spiritual Transformation* (New York: Avon, 2013).

Diane Stein, *Essential Reiki: A Complete Guide to an Ancient Healing Art* (Berkeley: Crossing Press, 1995).

Food and Nutrition

H. Byron Ballard, *Embracing Willendorf: A Witch's Way of Loving Your Body to Health and Fitness* (Asheville: Smith Bridge Press, 2017).

Jan Chozen Bays, *Mindful Eating: A Guide to Rediscovering a Healthy and Joyful Relationship with Food* (Boulder: Shambala Books, 2017).

Catherine Shanahan, *Deep Nutrition: Why Your Genes Need Traditional Food* (New York: Flatiron Books, 2018).

Michael Pollan, *Food Rules: An Eater's Manual* (London: Penguin Books, 2009).

Mark Hyman, *Food: What the Heck Should I Eat?* (New York: Little, Brown and Company, 2018).

Yoga and Tai Chi

Your best option for learning Yoga or Tai Chi is to find a local teacher. Your second-best option is to learn from videos. Gaia.com has a good selection of streaming video from a wide variety of teachers of both Yoga and Tai Chi. If you don't have the bandwidth for streaming, go to those sites to explore different teachers, then find those teachers' DVDs. Your local library may have some as well. Here are a few books that can also help you get started.

Dr. Paul Lam and Nancy Kaye, *Tai Chi for Beginners and the 24 Forms* (Sydney: Tai Chi Productions, 2006).

Robert Chuckrow, *The Tai Chi Book: Refining and Enjoying a Lifetime of Practice* (Wolfeboro: YMAA Press, 1998).

Phil Robinson, *Tai Chi: The Way of Balance in an Unbalanced World* (Bloomington: AuthorHouse, 2011).

Ken Cohen, *The Way of Qigong: The Art and Science of Chinese Energy Healing* (New York: Wellspring/Ballantine, 1999).

Yang Jwing-Ming and Thomas Gutheil, *The Root of Chinese Qigong: Secrets of Health, Longevity, & Enlightenment* (Wolfeboro: YMAA Publication Center, 2016).

Sri Swami Satchidananda, *Integral Yoga Hatha* (Buckingham: Integral Yoga Publications, 2002).

T. K. V. Desikachar, *The Heart of Yoga: Developing a Personal Practice* (Rochester: Inner Traditions, 1999).

Tara Fraser, *Total Yoga: A Step-By-Step Guide to Yoga at Home for Everybody* (London: Duncan Baird, 2007).

Donna Farhi, *Yoga Mind, Body & Spirit: A Return to Wholeness* (New York: Holt Paperbacks, 2011).

Breathwork

Donna Farhi, *The Breathing Book: Good Health and Vitality Through Essential Breath Work* (New York: Holt Paperbacks, 1996).

Richard Brown, M.D., and Patricia Gerbarg, M.D., *The Healing Power of the Breath: Simple Techniques to Reduce Stress and Anxiety, Enhance Concentration, and Balance Your Emotions* (Boulder: Shambala Publications, 2012).

Richard Rosen and Rodney Yee, *The Yoga of Breath: A Step-by-Step Guide to Pranayama* (Boulder: Shambala Publications, 2002).

Sri Swami Satchidananda, *The Breath of Life: Integral Yoga Pranayama: Step-by-Step Instructions in the Yogic Breathing Practices* (Buckingham: Integral Yoga Publications, 2015).

Mental Health

Top 25 Helpline Resources from The National Alliance on Mental Illness (NAMI) https://bit.ly/2wfaXGE (Accessed February 16, 2019)

CHAPTER TEN
Beltane—The Spring/ Summer Midpoint

It is an urge that can take us to the heart of the sublime or to the depths of depravity. Without it, life as we know it would not exist. While parts of it are exclusively physical, it resonates like a chorus of church bells through all the subtle levels of our reality. And Beltane, the spring/summer midpoint, is one of the best times to celebrate it.

Sex is, of course, what keeps life going above the level of the more primitive lifeforms. As the Sun strengthens here in the Northern Hemisphere, sex is happening everywhere (much to the distress of those of us who suffer from pollen allergies).

But, as important as the continuation of life is, sex serves more purposes than reproduction for humans. Sex is inextricably tied into our emotional lives, especially that emotion we call love, though we use it to express anger, fear, and various forms of emotional neediness as well. But under the right circumstances, sex—partnered or solo—can be a deeply spiritual experience, connecting us to another, larger reality that is essentially indescribable because it exists outside of the physical plane. It's the reality from whence we came. This connection to a larger reality is why sex is considered a powerful tool of manifestation in most magical systems. Good sex, focused on a goal, sends fireworks of intention out into the subtle realms, drawing in aligned energies and helping them crystallize into the world of five senses, the world in which we live.

Since it is such a powerful force, sex can also amplify abuse and trauma, and that resonates on the subtle planes as well, putting its negative stamp most egregiously on the victims but also on the underlying consciousness of our whole culture. No act of abuse goes unnoticed in this creative universe of ours, and we carry energetic imprints of anger, abuse, and trauma from life-time to lifetime until we are finally able to heal it. Fortunately, sex can also be a powerful method of healing, but it's one most of us have learned to block, to one degree or another, because of social and religious taboos. These taboos affect our whole body, causing emotional repression and physical armoring. (See Boadella's book in the resources section at the end of this chapter referencing Wilhelm Reich and "orgone" for more info on armoring.) Taboos about sexuality and our bodies can also cause energetic blockages in the area of the lower chakras with cascading effects throughout the whole body.

Don't make the mistake of thinking that because you have identified and understood the taboos and blockages intellectually you have freed yourself of them. There is a lot of social imprinting that occurs while we are quite young, and the only way to release that imprinting is to feel your way through it. It's important to reexperience it—however briefly, seconds can be enough—and release it from the level at which it was imprinted, keeping in mind that level is way more experiential than mental when you are young. We can clear a lot of this imprinting simply by letting ourselves allow and experience pleasure, not necessarily sexual pleasure, because there are so many taboos around sex, particularly shame-based taboos. From what I've read, heard, and experienced, not many people actually let down all their psychological barriers to pleasure during sex. Sure, they may enjoy it, even reach orgasm, but energetically, they don't open up to the possibilities of ecstatic connection to another person and/or to an expanded reality of joy and love.

The combination of social and personal taboos around sex are deep and strong, even when we intellectually recognize the possibilities, many people simply can't get past the energetic imprints in their body. Many imprints were taken on in childhood, but shaming, physical and emotional trauma, and repressive cultural attitudes affect adults as well, reinforcing the patterns established when they were young. There's a strong Puritanical strain in Western culture that is only emphasized by the overt sexualization of almost everything in advertising, more often than not reflecting a cultural obsession—a reaction to repression rather than a healthy interest. This isn't true of everyone, of course, but it's an attitude endemic in our culture.

It's important to learn to identify and release our blocks around experiencing pleasure. After all, if we are learning to create consciously, most of us would prefer to create a reality in which we experience pleasure—however we may define that—rather than hatred, anger, pain, trauma, etc. Learning to take pleasure in our bodies, whether by sex, or food, or touch, or experiencing the beauty and wonder of Nature, shifts our experience of life and helps heal the wounds that keep us from exploring the many creative possibilities our soul can envision. I think one of the best ways to explore pleasure and heal old pain and trauma is through connecting with Nature.

I have loved Earth and Nature since I was a very small child. Loved madly, passionately, completely. I have loved when I was in ecstatic communion with trees or the ocean, and loved still through bouts of poison ivy, bee stings, and hurricanes. I loved studying Nature's inner workings in the laboratory and loved it when I was trancing out dancing around a bonfire by a lake on a starry night. I loved swimming in Gardiner's Bay on Long Island as a child, and, as a young woman, after I finally got away from the forest of concrete that is my hometown (Manhattan), I loved exploring the neighborhood woods in Maryland on my old mare Leo and learning to tend a garden, both from people who had been tending gardens all their lives and from the classes I was taking on soil science, botany, and entomology. I love Nature still as an elder, firmly ensconced and gardening madly for many years on my mostly forested land halfway up a mountain in Western North Carolina.

I think many, if not most, of us experience this longing to connect with Nature in an intimate and intense manner. A big part of my spiritual practice is trying to reach "beginner's mind" with Nature, inviting back the perceptions and awareness of my preverbal self before I learned the labels for things. I think this is the easiest way for many of us to get out of our heads and reach that experiential level we knew in childhood again but this time with an adult's brain and perceptive abilities. Also, the natural world carries its own energy that can help free us from embedded patterns of pain and trauma.

There are other things you can do to help with breaking through old, deeply ingrained taboos and other patterns of energy. Those energies have a physical manifestation, and any protocol that works on a physical level to shift energetic patterns—acupuncture, Yoga, Tai Chi, Qigong, certain types of massage, certain types of dance, good sex—will help you shift and change those patterns on a physical level.

The spring/summer midpoint, a.k.a. Beltane (Beltane is celebrated April 30/May 1; the exact midpoint is around May 5), is an excellent time to focus on your body, both for health and pleasure. Learning to fully experience pleasure is an important aspect of spiritual growth, and sexual pleasure is a good place to start for most of us. Unfortunately, the sexual urge has been subject to varying degrees of social repression for centuries, using techniques that range from wildly funny, like some of the Victorian-era contraptions meant to prevent men from masturbating, to truly horrific practices such as female genital mutilation.

Why do we do this? Why do we repress this natural desire? The answer to that question is layered and complex, but I suspect that the repression has a lot to do with our human need to control anything we perceive as powerful. To reclaim that power for ourselves, we must sort through our beliefs about pleasure and sexuality and discard any unhealthy, socially imposed ones that do not align with who and what we want to be. Our bodies are treasures, the proverbial temple of our souls, and we are embodied for a reason.

⊣ KISS THE SKY ⊢

What's Your Pleasure?

Write out a list of things you find pleasurable, especially from a physical perspective. You'll work with this list in the Touch the Earth section. And it will be a work in progress. You can add to it and subtract from it as you become more aware of and discriminating about what brings you pleasure. (Personally, I'm still trying to convince myself that double-chocolate chip ice cream isn't the nectar of the gods.)

Discover Your Beliefs

Journal about your conscious and unconscious beliefs about pleasure. The conscious ones shouldn't be too hard to find. Just think of what your answer would be if someone asked you, "Is it OK to relax into pleasurable experiences or is it self-indulgent, dangerous, or just plain bad and wrong? If so, why? If not, why not?"

Those last two questions—why and why not—will give you some insight into your unconscious beliefs if you keep asking them until you've come to a core belief. For instance, let's say you feel that relaxing into pleasure can be dangerous. But you aren't sure why. So you start to think about it.

Maybe the answer doesn't come to you right away (this is a good time to ask your ancestors/helping spirits/Greater Self for insights), but eventually you remember that your grandmother always told you, "The devil finds work for idle hands," and you have strong placements in Taurus in your chart. That means idleness is one of your core competencies. It's not that you don't work hard or have a strong work ethic—you definitely do—but you treasure your idle time when you can just relax and enjoy life. Always have, always will. Grandma probably harangued you about the devil for that very reason.

"But I don't even believe in the devil!" you think. "That can't be why I think pleasure is dangerous." And this is where you really start excavating your beliefs and the emotional shifts they cause. You're going to find conflicting ones. For instance, you don't believe in the devil but you still are vaguely haunted by fear of an inchoate evil that could pounce on you at any time. Though it's not a belief you are fully conscious of, when you quietly and thoroughly examine your emotional state, you discover that underlying fear and anxiety. You may remember feeling it more acutely as a child, fear that you might be turned to the devil's purpose.

Now you could go deeper here and examine your beliefs about evil ("What is it? What causes it? Is it inherent in life, in us, or can we escape it?"). Or you might go right to, "No. I know better. I know the universe is based on a love that is stronger than any evil," either because you've thought this through before or you've had a peak experience, a direct download from a greater Mind that convinced you. Sit with this knowledge for a while. Let yourself feel the emotions it brings up. Explore the logical ramifications of your beliefs about idleness and pleasure and evil. As you do this, allow the unreasonable fears and their associated beliefs to dissipate under the illumination of the solid core beliefs you hold about the ultimate creative and loving nature of the universe.

You'll need to do this more than once before Grandma's judgments release their hold on you. But this kind of belief work is critical if you are going to grow into an independent human being aware of your connection to "life, the universe, and everything" while making decisions from a conscious, creative place within yourself instead of being driven by unconscious fears.

It's not that your unconscious disappears or no longer influences you. To the contrary—it is like the ocean, always mysterious, deep, ever-changing, full of monsters and miracles. But when you know the ways of the ocean and understand the winds, when you have the good ship of your mind and the stars of spirit to steer by, you can go places you've never been before. So think, journal, learn all you can about your unconscious and your mind. Then take your ship out of the harbor and explore, putting your thoughts and ideas into practice.

Honoring Your Body

Consider your beliefs about bodies in general. Do you believe a body is the vehicle of a soul in this lifetime? If we have any choice about the bodies we are born into, why do some of us choose to be born disabled in some way? Why is illness such a problem in this world?

As you think about these things, keep in mind the creative nature of the universe. Think about the fact that the bigger picture is never going to be entirely visible to us. Then, if you believe the body is the vehicle of the soul, if you believe in a creative universe, think about how you can honor your soul by honoring your body and by fully accepting it as your soul's creation, no matter its state of health. Acceptance doesn't mean you are OK with ill health or any problems you have with your body. Acceptance means an emotional state of awareness and understanding that this is where you are right now. Acceptance helps you release rage, grief, and anger so you can plan for the future and be energetically open to healing. Rage, grief, and anger are highly motivating but also highly restrictive emotions that are meant to be acknowledged and released within a relatively short time frame, not hung on to for years. Releasing them shifts the energy of your subtle bodies so they are more open to receiving healing.

Since you can't see the whole picture from your Greater Self's point of view, you can't fully understand what your soul is trying to create. You can't be sure of how your health fits into the bigger picture of your soul's growth and our co-creative endeavor here on Earth. But you do have choices to make every moment of every day about how you treat your body. Treating your body well must start with acceptance of where your body is now.

One way to reach a state of acceptance is to notice how often you think critically of your body and change those thought patterns. Check your criticisms against your beliefs about the body, the soul, and the creative nature of the universe. Notice the conflicting beliefs that are in play. Spend some time tracing your criticisms and insecurities back to their origins in your childhood. Choose which beliefs you want to claim. Then come up with a sentence that reflects your preferred beliefs and repeat it whenever you catch yourself beating yourself up about your body.

My personal preferred affirmation is simply "Walk in Beauty" because it reminds me of both the poem by Lord Byron, and the Navajo prayer:

> In beauty I walk
> With beauty before me I walk
> With beauty behind me I walk
> With beauty above me I walk
> With beauty around me I walk
> It has become beauty again[13]

Find something that is meaningful to you. If something doesn't come to you, ask your guides and ancestors for help, then watch for the synchronicities or inspirations that come to you.

⊣ TOUCH THE EARTH ⊢

Take a Walk

I probably don't even need to tell you to get outside when spring is turning to summer! As usual, be observant. Note what is growing, what is flowering, where Sun is rising, and how it rises a little earlier and a little further north every day.

---

13. "Walk In Beauty: Prayer From The Navajo People." Talking Feather, https://talking-feather.com/home/walk-in-beauty-prayer-from-navajo-blessing/.

Enjoy and Observe

Do something you enjoy doing and allow yourself to savor it. Give it your full focus and attention. Then watch for any conflicting beliefs that come up about whether or not it's OK to experience this pleasure. We often hold ourselves back from pleasure for all sorts of reasons. Actually doing those things you enjoy and paying attention to your thoughts and emotions when you're doing them will help you identify those underlying, usually unconscious reasons and determine whether or not they are valid. You'll also become far more aware of the fine line between true enjoyment and overindulgence. (I usually discover that at the halfway line on a pint of ice cream.)

Change Your Focus

Make a point of finding at least some enjoyment in whatever it is you are doing. You may not be able to affect the traffic on your commute, but you can change your attention, awareness, and attitude. Instead of putting all your focus on how awful the traffic is, listen to music, do some breathing exercises, pick an issue that is currently impacting your life and see if you can brainstorm three completely new ways to deal with that issue. You can also simply choose to be fully present in the traffic, putting your complete attention on your current sensory input. That is, in fact, the beginning of a little spell I use to influence my path through traffic, but just practice being present in it for now.

Ritual of Realignment

Here's a little ritual you can do to cleanse your subtle bodies of any stagnant energy and realign your energy with the changing seasons. Give yourself at least an hour and a half for this, plus any travel time—it's not something that can be rushed.

Take a salt bath. Put 1–2 cups of minimally processed salt—coarse sea salt is ideal—in a tub of water. There are herbs and stones that can be used effectively to amp up cleansing baths—you can learn more about them in books on cleansing in chapter 6. I like to add a few drops of lavender essential oil to my bath, but salt alone will do the trick very well for now, especially if you make a little ritual of it. Light a candle before you get in the bath. Call on any spirit allies or deities you work with. (If you aren't acquainted with any yet, just call on your Greater Self.)

Soak for at least fifteen minutes but no more than thirty. Submerge your head at least three times. Stay in a meditative state—no washing or grooming. Just focus on your breathing and feel your personal energy shift. Imagine your subtle bodies strengthening, shining brightly, and breaking through any negativity you may have picked up. The salt helps in this process, breaking up stagnant, problematic energies in need of recycling. (If you don't have a bathtub, use a large bucket of salt water in the shower, pouring it over yourself with a pitcher, head to toe.)

When you feel "done," pull the plug and sit there as the water drains away. Now, you can shower and wash. At least rinse and dry with a clean towel. Dress in loose, comfortable clothing suitable for sitting on the ground, or at your altar if you can't get outdoors.

Go to a favorite spot out in nature where you will be undisturbed or sit down at your altar. If you're at your altar, you'll need to identify a spot in nature for yourself so you can imagine it in a meditation. You might want to light candles and incense and put out a bowl of fresh water. If you can get a little bit of earth or a rock from the spot you'll be imagining, that would be ideal. If you are outdoors, you have sunshine (even if it's behind clouds) and fresh air, plants, and the earth beneath your feet. Breath and acknowledge these things.

Make an offering to the spirits of this place. (We'll discuss the whys and wherefores of offerings in the next chapter.) On my own land, I'll leave some kind of food. Often milk and honey, eggs, fruits, or grains. The raccoons and possums and snakes and foxes and other wildlife will clean it up, usually overnight. I have a little stone altar near the stream in my backyard where I leave offerings. Dishes of liquid or honey can drown insects, so I pour them out on to the ground or onto the altar stone. In a park or public land, I would make an offering of plain water and a bit of cornmeal because you don't want to attract or feed the wildlife on public lands, and cornmeal is an excellent non-burning, non-toxic fertilizer for whatever plants are there. Do not offer anything that is not biodegradable, and keep the offerings small.

If you are indoors, envision yourself there, but prepare the actual offerings and have them on your altar along with an empty bowl to receive them.

Stand quietly, offerings in hand. Come into the present moment. Be aware of how this place affects all your senses. Say (out loud) something like the following:

> I call to the spirits of this place, to the spirits of this land, and give thanks for your presence and blessings in my life.
>
> I offer this [name the offering here; e.g., "water and corn-meal"] in gratitude for the beauty and wonder of this place. I give offering and thanks to you in all your forms.

Then leave the offerings. If you are at your altar, put the offerings in a bowl. Ideally, you will later take them to the actual place and leave them there, but if you can't do that, dispose of them in a compost pile, under a tree somewhere, in a river, or even in a potted plant (in which case I'd definitely suggest limiting it to cornmeal and water). Also, I should probably note that more is not necessarily better. Don't leave so much of whatever you are offering that it causes disruption to the local ecosystem—or the potted plant.

Now choose a spot to sit (or stand) and meditate. (If you are at your altar, do this in vision.) Sit facing one of the four primary directions—whichever one feels right to you (if you really aren't sure, pick north). You can use the compass on your phone, or simply judge which direction you are facing by the position of Sun. Settle in to a comfortable posture. Bring your attention fully into the present moment and focus on your breath. Let your breath descend into your belly. Let it adjust naturally until you are breathing in a full but relaxed manner. Close your eyes. (If you are doing this work in vision, your eyes are already closed. You should now close your eyes in the vision as well.)

Now sense a ray of red energy extending from the base of your spine, down through the Earth, all the way to the molten core of the planet. Let the energy flow freely. This is your connection to the planet, and you can release energy into the central fire at the core while drawing up what you need, reinvigorating your subtle bodies with the raw power of the planet itself. This cord, this connection, should always be there, whether or not you are actively working with it. It is your anchor to the planet, and you can visualize it and consciously pull more strength and energy into you when you are in need of it.

Once you have established your awareness of the Earth cord, turn your attention to the sky above you and to the top of your skull, the fontanel, that "soft spot" on a baby's skull, the seventh chakra. About a foot above that spot, see a diamond-clear nexus of energy that draws in energy from the stars and funnels it into your seventh chakra, then down through your spine, changing colors as it descends through your chakras, until it meets with the incoming red energy and intertwines with it. Envision yourself connected to both earth and sky, the energy from both flowing freely.

Your chakras modulate that energy, and if you've done some reading about them, you may want to work with them consciously now. Sometimes old fears, even past life ones, and externally imposed beliefs that chafe your soul will weaken, restrict, or distort a particular chakra. You'll need to work with this carefully to shift the energy and restore the free flow of prana. Remember as you work with your chakras that you are looking for balance, not drilling for oil. It's very rare that you need to bust through an energetic blockage. Usually, dissolving or unraveling it little by little, using the energy of earth and sky, will do the best job of bringing that chakra back to health and balance.

Instead of restriction, you may find that a particular area feels as though it is weak and wobbly. It may have been blown open by too strong a flow of energy in the past. The same energy, directed by your mind, can be used to help that chakra find its proper pattern, and help it regain strength and stability.

Whether you are working with your chakras or just with the flow of energy, notice where the blockages and other problems are without trying to force any change. Sense the strong vortex of life and growth around and flowing through you and let it work its healing magic. When you feel comfortable and connected, open your eyes. (If you are doing this in front of your altar in visionary journey, you will keep your physical eyes closed throughout. Open your eyes in your vision.)

Look at what is in your field of vision. Look with your full attention. Look, listen, smell, feel, and let your sixth sense explore as well. Just be there and aware. At some point, ask to be shown what you can do to deepen your relationship with the natural world, and with this place in particular. The answer may not come to you right away, but it should become clear over the next two or three days.

When the ritual feels complete, walk around a bit to ground yourself back in ordinary reality. Before you leave, thank the spirits of the place and check to make sure you have not left anything behind, then head on home or bring your consciousness back to your altar space.

Connecting with nature in that manner brings us back into harmony with the world around us. You can do this ritual at any time of year, but the energies of Beltane are highly active and easily felt, so this is a good time to begin.

Resources

Melanie Marquis, *Beltane: Rituals, Recipes & Lore for May Day* (St. Paul: Llewellyn Publications, 2015).

Stella Resnick, *The Pleasure Zone: Why We Resist Good Feelings & How to Let Go and Be Happy* (Newburyport: Conari Press, 1997).

Alexander Lowen, *Pleasure: A Creative Approach to Life* (Hinesburg: Lowen Foundation, 2013).

Barbara Holland, *Endangered Pleasures: In Defense of Naps, Bacon, Martinis, Profanity, and Other Indulgences* (New York: William Morrow, 2000).

Christopher Ryan and Cacilda Jetha, *Sex at Dawn: How We Mate, Why We Stray, and What It Means for Modern Relationships* (New York: Harper Perennial, 2011).

Sheri Winston, CNM, RN, BSN, LMT, *Women's Anatomy of Arousal: Secret Maps to Buried Pleasure* (Miami: Mango Garden Press, 2010).

Jason Miller, *Sex, Sorcery, and Spirit* (Newburyport: Weiser Books, 2014).

Margo Anand, *The Art of Sexual Ecstasy: The Path of Sacred Sexuality for Western Lovers* (New York: Jeremy P. Tarcher, 1989).

Wendy Maltz, *The Sexual Healing Journey: A Guide for Survivors of Sexual Abuse* (New York: William Morrow Paperbacks, 2012).

Naomi Ardea, *The Art of Healing from Sexual Trauma: Tending Body and Soul through Creativity, Nature, and Intuition* (Minneapolis: Wise Ink Creative Publishing, 2016).

David Boadella, *Wilhelm Reich: The Evolution of His Work* (Washington: Regnery Publishing, 1974).

Animism, Gods, and Offerings

Did you feel a little silly or uncomfortable when you left the offering in the Beltane ritual? Maybe your inner child was loving it but a parental voice in your head was saying something like, "This is ridiculous. Why are you playing at this fantasy?" or, "What's the point? Waste of time!" Or maybe you just decided to skip the whole thing.

That's OK. What matters here is that you are honest with yourself about how you felt when you did or thought about doing that ritual. Because when you sort out all your feelings on the subject, there will almost certainly be a part of you wondering if spirits are real. If they are, then leaving offerings for them is a whole different action than leaving offerings for something you believe is, at best, a psychological construct that only exists in your head. So let's take a look at the logic behind the practice of offerings and exactly who we are making these offerings to. Then your logical, rational self can sit back in its easy chair with an adult beverage, relaxing and observing while you are doing ritual instead of scoffing and critiquing and generally interfering in the process.

Consciousness: Finding Bedrock

We begin our exploration of the spirit world on the foundation of Consciousness. Which is, admittedly, not much of a foundation as we think of foundations because Consciousness is truly infinite—much more than we can even begin to wrap our minds around. We're limited in our understanding of reality, but that doesn't mean we can't find some philosophical bedrock to build our lives on.

Bedrock lies at different depths at different places on Earth, and the same is true of our philosophies. Some people need to dig more deeply than others to find their bedrock. Many people build on the relatively shallow bedrock of whatever religion they grew up with. Others dig a little deeper, finding another religion that answers the big questions for them and building there. My philosophical bedrock is a Consciousness that creates and fully inhabits every molecule, atom, or subatomic particle of physical reality, and that, though I will never fully understand it, still supports and holds me in all my creative endeavors.

One of the reasons many of us find this idea of Consciousness so hard to grasp is that we are in the habit of thinking of it in exclusively human terms, as a level of self-awareness that appears to be unique to humans. It's hard enough for us to comprehend and deal with the fact that other people's minds don't necessarily work the way ours do. The concept of many different types of consciousness—say, the consciousness of a squirrel, or a horse, or an ant—is so foreign to our Western way of thinking that, for centuries, most people, certainly the Christian church, denied that animals had consciousness at all, much less a soul. Materialist scientists, of course, denied the existence of a soul at all, and many suggested animals could not feel pain.

But that is changing. Quite a few experiments have been done just in the past couple of decades that support not only the existence of consciousness in animals, but the fact that they communicate, have relationships, and interact intelligently with their environment. Some, like monkeys and crows, even make tools.

More science happened, and, hey, it looks like plants have a form of consciousness too, communicating with each other about various threats, forming communities that react to each individual, even supporting sick neighbors.

And what about rocks?

Wait a minute! Let's not go overboard here. Rocks aren't conscious. That's all in the fervid imaginations of New Age crystal-clutchers.

Right?

Is it?

If we posit that Consciousness is both fully immanent and transcendent, then yes, rocks have some form of consciousness as well. So do bits of dust or grains of sand. It's hard to imagine what that kind of consciousness must be like, isn't it? It's tempting to think that a mote of dust or a grain of sand must not be aware, but we don't know that. Perhaps their consciousness is completely focused on resonance, or on the ever-changing spin of the electrons and sub-atomic particles that make up their reality, something we are aware of through our tools and equations but cannot experience directly. Certainly, it seems that we are going to have to do some rethinking of what consciousness is (not that we've ever been able to define it adequately in the first place).

Now let's go in the other direction. Could there be consciousnesses that are larger and more aware of the ultimate nature of reality than we are? Is it possible that there are consciousnesses that are not fully focused in this physical realm, but still have an interest in or connection to it? Heck, is it possible that there are many other realms—some physical as we understand it, some not—in which Consciousness creates?

It strikes me as being not only possible but likely. And my personal adventures in Consciousness, along with those of many others, have lead me to believe that those larger consciousnesses not only exist but that it is possible to communicate with them. In fact, there appears to be a profusion of non-physical beings who interact with this dimension of reality but are not fully present within it in physical form. Some of them have a type of consciousness close enough to our own that it is possible for us to communicate.

The nature of Consciousness is essentially creative, and there will always be new frontiers to explore. But that doesn't mean we can't get a better grip on how to create—and improve—the reality we experience and learn to communicate better with other forms of Consciousness while gaining a deeper understanding of the universe and the loving Consciousness—from which we are in no way separate, remember—that drives it.

You may come to a different conclusion, but I was convinced long ago that the universe is moving inexorably toward love—its basic trajectory, its mission, is creative—and since we are part of it, we get to explore whatever we can conceive of creating. Some of what we have created is pretty awful; some of it is sublime. But all that we create is contained within a greater love that is the essence of All That Is, of Consciousness. We have, at least on the level of our Greater Selves, free will to create as we choose—no other option would be a loving one. Love is inseparable from creativity.

If we know love is there, know it in our hearts, know that we are part of it and our souls can never be separated from it, then we can release the existential fear and the need to control. That is a lengthy process—the work of a lifetime—but the world opens up as we work through the process of reconnection to love and to our own creative power. It's easier to connect with gods and spirits when we are confident of our place in the universe, confident that we are loved and part of a community of larger consciousnesses. When we get to know that community, then they can guide us in the direction we want to go while helping us learn to create with more power and skill from within physical reality.

Spirit beings are not all gods—not by a long shot—but some of them are, and by "gods" I mean beings of expanded consciousness and power, who, as part of their own growth and development, are involved in the evolution of Earth and its lifeforms. There are numerous beings that are nonphysical but still attached to the physical realm through patterns of emotion and consciousness. These include (but are not limited to) human ancestors, souls between lives, various spirits of place, tutelary spirits such as angels and guides, and overlighting spirits of plants and animals. What we can perceive with our five senses is far less than what is there. (A basic scientific knowledge of spectrums of light and sound tell us this is true.) But the experience of many tells us that we can expand our awareness beyond our five senses and communicate with beings who do not fully share our physical world. We can learn to tune the radio dial of our mind to pick up other signals, signals from the spirit world.

For most of us, doing so takes focus and persistence. There is what is often called a "veil" between the worlds of spirit and physical reality. It's there for a reason. For us to create freely within the realm of time and space, we must know what it is like to be bound by it. We must understand and respect its limits. We must be fully focused here, part and parcel of this world, which is not to say there are not channels of communication between the two worlds. We can access those channels and part the veil through meditation, trancework, altars, and offerings. A good place to start is by connecting with the natural world.

Animism

Let's step outside now, and briefly explore the ideas of animism, the belief that Spirit—Consciousness—inhabits every aspect of our world. We'll look into the spirits of Nature, an important aspect of animism, in more detail in chapter 13.

Whether I am watering my houseplants, working in my garden, or sitting with my feet in the stream that flows through my backyard, I greet spirits—spirits of the plants, of the stream, of the trees and rocks, and the overlighting spirits of the place. Sometimes, I sit near my little stream, close my eyes, and connect with various spirits, often the spirit of the mountain I live on. I believe that communication between us occurs, and I often ask for advice from local spirits on the regional ecology and the care and feeding of my land, or simply commune and request their blessing.

There are different forms of consciousness that inhabit and influence our world, particularly the natural world. Trees, for instance, have unique consciousnesses, but what about the forest? Does the whole forest have its own consciousness? If rivers have their own consciousness, is it the same at the source as it is at the delta? When I drive Route 81 between my home in North Carolina and points north I sense a dragon-like being who seems to me to be the living spirit of these ancient Appalachian Mountains. Does this being's awareness extend all through the range (which runs all the way to Scotland) or is it limited to a specific area? Or is it my perception that is limited?

These spirits I commune with appear to me as sentient—aware, responsive, reactive—to one degree or another, so let's consider this question of sentience and how we get from Consciousness—the fabric of the universe, All That Is, the consciousness in every atom, every mote of dust—to the kind of individual, separate consciousness that we recognize and can communicate with. I have to admit, I don't have any solid answers, just some ideas that have come to me through reading and meditation. Here's a metaphor to express how I'm currently viewing it. Remember, it's only a metaphor, but it gives some insight.

In the same way that a zygote—the first cell of a new organism, formed by the fusion of two gametes—has within it the DNA of both parents, combined in a way that will develop into a unique being, so can consciousnesses combine to form a whole new consciousness that then also develops from a "consciousness zygote" into a new individual along unique lines that are directed by the "DNA" of both parents.

Cells multiply and differentiate to form various organs and structures of the human body, and the environment also affects development. A consciousness zygote also grows from what is apparently a barely sentient collection of "cells"—tiny units of consciousness—into a functioning being with levels of awareness comparable to those of its parents. Our bodies develop, change, age, die, and are recycled. Perhaps the same is true of consciousnesses.

The problem with this metaphor, of course, is that physical bodies develop through time, while Consciousness is the creator of time itself and not bound by it. Our consciousnesses may develop along with our bodies as we travel through time, but these spirits we are talking about are essentially nonphysical (though they may have anchors in the physical world) and—at least some to some degree—are not bound by time and space. What about them?

Sit and meditate on how it might feel to exist outside of time, without space. Think about the vast reaches of our universe, the minuscule particles of an atom. As big and as small as our universe is, there is something more that transcends it.

You may start feeling a little dizzy, confused, or unmoored. It's OK. We are meant to be within time and space, and grokking its lack is not something we do easily. But if you work with this meditation for a while, what you can take away from it is a big dose of awe and wonder, a healthy dash of humility, and gratitude for your part in this amazing creation. Keep in mind that the basic spin of the universe is toward love, even though, like a retrograde planet, it sometimes seems to be heading in the opposite direction. But—also like a retrograde planet—that perception is an illusion.

When you return from your meditation, spend a few moments grounding and centering yourself back in time and space. Touch the ground, or the floor if you can't get outside. Run some cool water over your hands. Take a few deep breaths and know that you are held and loved here within time and space.

Now, with this expanded perspective, let's get back to the question of sentience. The zygote-to-adult metaphor, while flawed, is a useful perspective for us since our consciousness is currently hard-wired into time and space.

If you accept that Consciousness is more spacious and varied than you can possibly comprehend, if you accept that it is creative in its essence, then it's not that big a leap to the idea that there are many, many different forms of Consciousness, some of which are not tied within time and space, some of which are aware of a far larger reality than we are.

Animism says that Consciousness is everywhere—in rocks, in streams and trees, in every facet of Nature. Spirit is entwined in every manifestation within time and space. Learning to communicate with different consciousnesses—communing with a stream or tree or the spirit of a forest is a skill that develops with practice and an open mind. While the word wasn't coined until the nineteenth century, the concept of animism is very, very old, and thoroughly cross-cultural. In animistic societies, learning to communicate with non-human consciousnesses began in childhood. Most of us raised in Western civilization did not have this advantage. But you can learn. I hope you will. I think you'll find your life is greatly enriched by the effort.

Offerings

Offerings are important when working with the gods and other beings of spirit, so let's get into the concept of offerings and why we would make them. Invariably, when I bring up the topic in a class, someone asks, "Why can't I just do this with meditation and trancework? They're spirits, right? Why do I need to have all this physical stuff?"

Yes, they're spirits, but you aren't. When you bring physical stuff to the relationship, you open the channel from the physical side and give spirits something to home in on. Offerings are like a beacon. They also bring with them (or should) your personal energy of introduction and respect. If you were at a social event and wanted to meet someone you knew about and respected but had never met, you would introduce yourself politely, see if they were open to chatting with you, then spend some time getting to know them. You wouldn't shout across the room, "Hey, you, come on over here! I've got some questions for you and some work I need you to do for me." First, you need to make the connection, and then you can work to expand it.

This is why we use both focused mental work and physical offerings—they help us make the introduction and keep the channels of communication open once the introduction has been made. They also give a being of spirit an anchor into this realm, a place to sit, as it were, and work with you in your world.

I don't approach offerings as tit-for-tat or payment for services performed. (Though, admittedly, many do, and some spirits are happy to barter.) I see them as a gift, given with love, respect, and gratitude to a remarkable being who has chosen to be present and ally themselves with me, to help and guide me. These beings have their own reasons for doing this, some of which we come to understand, some of which we will never know. I'd suggest that you not go into this sort of interaction with a transactional mindset. Bring an offering to the altar as you might bring a bottle of wine to a gathering of friends—with anticipation of the interaction, respect for the people there, and with an open, generous heart.

One more thing to note about offerings is that it's the energy of the offerings that is "consumed" by the spirit, and what remains in place should be disposed of in as natural a way as possible. Your offerings should be biodegradable and so can be poured on the ground, buried, composted, or put into a body of water—always with thought and care for its possible effects on the ecology. I strongly recommend against consuming the offering yourself. It was a gift. Let it go.

Finding Gods

When you think about the vastness of the universe, the possibilities of Consciousness, can you really convince yourself that humans are at the pinnacle? Doesn't it make sense that if we can imagine more, Consciousness has created far more than we can even imagine?

Some vast, complex consciousnesses are as different from our own as we are from a bacterium. They may be aware of us, but we can barely begin to comprehend what they are. Others, not quite as vast, still have a more expanded awareness of the process of creation than we do and levels of power within the physical realm that are not accessible to us. They are more human-like, more involved in our world, but they work on a much larger playing field, one that we can't see easily, if at all. You can call these beings whatever you choose, of course. I call them gods.

As you begin to interact with gods and spirits, it's important to remember that physical reality is not a lesser reality, and that you, too, are a spirit. Life is not a testing ground to determine whether or not we are good enough to get into heaven. We are here to learn to create within the limits of time and space. It's a challenging assignment we have chosen to take on, and the spirits who are associated with this realm also have their own creative endeavors they are pursuing, of which we may well be a part, with our Greater Self's knowledge and consent.

They interact with us for their own reasons, and often one of those reasons is because they like to share in the intensity of experience, perception, and emotion that is offered by creating within the boundaries of time and space. At least some of the gods and spirits who interact with us in the ongoing creation of physical reality have an interest in cooperating with us, guiding us, helping us. (And frankly, it seems we need all the help we can get.)

At the level of our Greater Self, we agreed to jump off the cloud into this lifetime, work to make the best of it, and take what comes. Like a deep-sea diver who jumps off a boat in the middle of the ocean, we have a boat anchored on the other side of the veil with a crew who has agreed to assist us in our incarnational endeavors. It's a good idea to make sure you have a clear line of communication to your crew if you want to make the most of this lifetime.

The crew is generally a motley bunch consisting of ancestors and various helpers and guides (we'll look at working with them in chapter 17) but there is at least one deity (quite possibly more) who has a long-term interest in you, perhaps through many or all your lifetimes. One who understands you on a soul level and sees what you are trying to accomplish. If you consciously search for those being(s), they will make themselves known to you. Once you've opened a line of communication, you'll have a hotline to advice and, often, concrete help in moving your life in the direction you want to go.

How do you connect with your gods? First, just ask. Sit at your altar, light some candles, and start by meditating on your core values. Make your basic moral and ethical choices clear to the universe. The gods you choose to work with may challenge those choices as your work together progresses, but if you are clear about your values, they will not betray them. Then say, in your own words, that you would like to open your life to guidance from a deity. (And yes, say it out loud.) Now just sit for a while, quieting your mind, opening to impressions, visions, and ideas. You may get something you can follow up on, or not. Don't worry about it; just be aware of what you're experiencing.

When you feel done, blow out the candles, journal about your experience, even if it didn't seem like much, then go about your life, remaining open to insights and synchronicities in the days and weeks ahead. Do some research on any gods who you become aware of by whatever means. Don't expect them to manifest in front of you, but if you see a picture of a statue of Athena on Facebook that draws you, or a book about Ganesha is sitting with the cover facing out as you are browsing a bookstore, or you have a dream about a chariot drawn by cats that is driven by a goddess, then you're probably being contacted and should follow up with more research.

Use the internet to explore some of your visions. For instance, if you saw a chariot drawn by cats in your meditations, plug that phrase into your favorite search engine and see what you find. This research is important, particularly when it comes to offerings and invocations. Think of what you'd do if you were sent to the airport to pick up someone you'd never met before. You'd probably carry a sign with their name on it so they could find you. Specific types of offerings, invocations, and mythology are all ways of carrying a sign for the deity you are trying to contact. Once you have a solid relationship with a deity, they may tell you they'd enjoy some other kind of offering or give you a new myth to contemplate. But at first, go with what's in the historical record until you are certain you've made the right connection.

This business of finding your gods is intuitive and magical. When you get the feeling that a particular being is reaching out to you, then reach back. Study their history, their myths, their likes and dislikes, the plants and animals that were associated with them, and how they interacted with humans and other deities. Print out a picture of them that appeals to you, write or find an invocation to them, put together an appropriate offering, and sit down at your altar. Light some candles and incense—preferably candles of a color and incense made from herbs that are associated with them. Say the invocation, make the offering. Then speak your heart. Tell them you would like to get to know them better. We'll be looking at more in-depth ways of communicating with spirits in chapter 17, but for now, just tell them you would like to get to know them and better understand them and the connection between you. Then just sit quietly and see what visions or insights come to you. Once you feel done, thank them and blow out the candles. Leave the offering on your altar for a while, but clear it away when it starts to decay. I usually go for twenty-four hours, but you may get an intuition about how long it should stay. In subsequent communion with them, if you feel welcomed, you may ask for their insights, help, and protection.

One thing you want to be cautious about is making sure the spirit you are interacting with is truly a deity, a divine one, and not some mischievous spirit masquerading as a deity. I suggest you work only with gods who have a historical record and call on them by name. Develop the relationship slowly and carefully, checking with your intuition, making sure you feel comfortable with this connection. Feel free to ask for some kind of confirmation that you are connected with the being you called on.

In the days that follow, if you get that help/information/understanding you need, if you sense an otherworldly protection, then repeat the invocation/offering sequence several times to deepen the relationship. You may want to use one or more of the techniques in chapter 17 to clarify your communications. If you don't feel that the connection is happening, then repeat the invocation/offering sequence, say that you thank them for their presence and attention, but don't feel like there is a connection. Ask, if you are wrong about that, to please let you know and say you will reconsider, but for now you will not be making any further attempts to connect. (Burn or bury the picture with respect. Don't just trash it.)

When you do find a deity with whom you connect, then consider getting a statue and perhaps making a little shrine for them. This is an ongoing, valuable relationship. Treat it as such. Statues, like offerings, are helpful in creating a connection between you and the deity. You are not worshiping the statue—you are offering the deity a home in your world.

I know all this may seem pretty outrageous to some of you, and some of you are doubtlessly murmuring about emotional regression and imaginary childhood friends, but put your skepticism aside for a little while. You can always pick it up again later. Play with the idea of nonphysical beings who can and do communicate with us. Open yourself to the possibility and see what happens.

Respect these beings and express your feelings of reverence and love, but don't subjugate yourself to them. The gods don't look down on the planet, see us poor, struggling humans, feel sorry for us (or not), and intervene occasionally just to stir the pot or get a sheep or a shot of booze as a sacrifice. The gods, like us, are involved in a multilayered, creative expression of Consciousness that involves manifesting Consciousness within the Consciousness-created framework of time and space.

Your life is a work of art, not a subject of pity. The gods are creators—and so are we. They are fulfilling their own need for expansion and growth in connection to our time and space reality, and so are we. We work, finely tuned, fully within a particular frequency of Consciousness that sets limits to see what might be created within those limits, like a painter limited by the dimensions of a canvas or a sculptor limited by a block of marble. The gods and spirits we work with have a more expanded awareness of reality and far fewer limits, but that means they can never fully experience physical reality as we do except as we choose to share with them. We do not go empty-handed into this relationship. We create together.

The farthest reaches and ramifications of Consciousness are way beyond our ability to fathom. But we can play with what we *can* fathom, what we *can* understand, and create in concert with other beings whose conscious reach is greater than our own, who can help us break through into new dimensions of consciousness, of creativity.

Your individual imagination plays a role in what you see because it opens the road to the spirit realm. The willingness and ability to extend your perception beyond your five senses into the imaginal realm is an essential first step. The individual spirit's intent and "personality" play a role as well. While some visions and/or communications are shared (such as apparitions of the Virgin Mary at Medjugorje and Fatima), most are personal and personalized. The fact that we may see the same spirit in different ways does not mean that we are fantasizing or hallucinating. The spirit realm is far more flexible than the physical, and far more varied. We'll talk about communicating with nonphysical beings in chapter 17, but for now, just spend some time contemplating the whole idea of spirits and see where it takes you, and, perhaps, who you sense might be making the effort to contact you.

When I went looking for bedrock, I found my gods. The life I have built on the foundation of their understanding and guidance allows me to learn, grow, create, connect, and weather life's inevitable storms.

Resources

Ivo Dominguez, Jr., *Spirit Speak: Knowing and Understanding Spirit Guides, Ancestors, Ghosts, Angels, and the Divine* (Newburyport: New Page Books, 2008).

Emma Restall Orr, *The Wakeful World: Animism, Mind and the Self in Nature* (London: Moon Books, 2012).

R. Ogilvie Crombie, *Encounters with Nature Spirits: Co-creating with the Elemental Kingdom* (Forres: Findhorn Press, 2018).

Christopher Penczak, *Spirit Allies: Meet Your Team from the Other Side* (Newburyport: Weiser Books, 2002).

S. Kelley Harrell, *Life Betwixt: Essays on Allies in the Everyday and Shamanism Among* (Fuquay Varina: Soul Intent Arts, 2016).

Janet and Stewart Farrar, *The Witches' Goddess* (Custer: Phoenix Publishing, 1987).

Janet and Stewart Farrar, *The Witches' God* (Custer: Phoenix Publishing, 1989).

CHAPTER TWELVE
Litha—Summer Solstice

It's the most wonderful time of the year! Yes, I know the Andy Williams song is about Yule, but though I enjoy both solstices, I admit summer is my favorite, if only because I love plants so much and summer is their big show-off season.

Litha, the Summer Solstice (a.k.a. Midsummer, Alban Hefin), falls right around June 21. It marks the maximum axial tilt of the North Pole toward the Sun and the longest day length in the Northern Hemisphere. Which means, of course, that from this day on until Yule, Sun will be in its waning phase, and we are moving into the dark half of the year. Right now, the balance of our awareness is fully "of Earth" but will begin to shift more into the world of spirit and away from the manifest world in the coming months.

But right this very moment, Sun is shining brightly, and plants are growing like crazy. Those two things are, of course, very much linked. That big, blazing nuclear reactor in the sky not only gives us warmth and light, but it is at the foundation of the Web of Life. Photosynthesis—the reaction that converts light, carbon dioxide, and water into the chemical energy of carbohydrates—drives the food chain on which we depend. The reaction also releases oxygen as a waste product, a rather useful byproduct for those of us who need to breathe the stuff.

Chlorophyll is the molecule at the heart of photosynthesis and is responsible for the coloration of green plants. Interestingly, the structure of the chlorophyll molecule is almost identical to the structure of the hemoglobin molecule.

The primary difference is that chlorophyll is built around an atom of magnesium, and hemoglobin—the substance in our blood that colors it red and carries oxygen—is built around an atom of iron. Red, of course, is the color that we use as a primary symbol of the Winter Solstice, while the Summer Solstice is a celebration of green. I don't discuss the magic of colors in this book, but color is an important part of magic, and you may find this bit of information about two of the most important biochemical processes on Earth useful when you're planning some magic.

Summer Solstice is a great time to get to know some of the spirits of the land and the spirits of the plants. How? Let's start with a walking meditation.

⊣ TOUCH THE EARTH ⊢

Finding Your Place

Do some exploring to find a place in Nature that intuitively calls to you as a place where you can do spiritual work. I'm not talking full-fledged ritual (though that would be great), just someplace where you can sit and meditate while surrounded by Nature. Make sure it's a place where you feel safe and will be relatively undisturbed. It should not be too far from your home. Even in the city there are parks nearby, but if you want to go to a more remote location, that's OK as long as you sense that you are in the same general land-area as your home. I can't tell you exactly how many miles that might be. You'll have to use and trust your intuition.

Finding this spot is a meditation in and of itself. You may know of several nearby areas that are candidates, or you could use Google Earth to find likely spots nearby. (It may also be that you already know the exact perfect spot but do this exercise anyway.) Identify at least three likely places, and over the course of a weekend or three, go to all those places and spend some time walking around. Bring a small container of cornmeal (or other environmentally appropriate offering), a water bottle, a small journal, and a pen with you. (Yes, you can use an app on your phone as a journal, but put your phone in airplane mode before starting this adventure.)

When you get there, begin by evaluating practical things like accessibility and safety. If those are adequate, then start walking around, getting a sense of how you feel here and how your feelings change as you move from one area to the next. For instance, if you are in a park with a large lake, being near the lake may make you feel expansive and inspired. Walking through a nearby stand of trees, you may feel watched—maybe in a loving way, maybe not.

Find a place where you can sit comfortably (preferably on a rock or on the earth itself but a park bench will do). There should be no obvious distractions in the form of other people too close by, machinery noises, loud music, etc. Begin your meditation on and communion with Nature by simply observing. Notice what's within your line of sight, what you hear, and what you smell. Touch the earth beneath you with your hands. As your mind quiets and you become more aware of your surroundings, notice what naturally draws your attention. It may be a tree, a rock, or a body of water. It could be a turtle, or a squirrel, or a hawk flying overhead. It may be a small plant or a natural arrangement of plants. With your mind quiet, with no judgment or concern about "doing it right," ask the object of your attention if they are willing to communicate with you.

If you sense agreement (don't sweat over whether what you sense is "real" —just trust your intuition) simply introduce yourself (you can do this entirely in your mind or out loud), and explain that you are learning to communicate with spirits of Nature. Respectfully ask if there is anything they would like you to know about them, and then listen.

Listening is the hardest part of this. Don't judge your perceptions. Just accept what comes to you. You may feel as though you are making it all up. It's possible that you are, to one degree or another. It takes practice to learn to distinguish the signal from the noise, but it's almost certain you will get at least some of the signal. Journal about your perceptions immediately afterward. Also note down your observations of what is going on in nature—the weather, animals you saw, etc.

Repeat this practice at the other two places you've chosen and decide if you would like to do this kind of work regularly at all three places or get to know one of them in depth. (If you have any time constraints, I suggest choosing just one.) Come to one of your places whenever you want to do some of the exercises suggested in the books below, when you feel the need for an energetic reset, or for any kind of Earth-based meditation. But do make it a regular part of your spiritual practice. Get it on the calendar or go when your fancy takes you. Try to go once a month at the least. If you don't think you can do that, then find a place closer to home. Regular interaction with Nature and the planet is a prerequisite for full mental and spiritual health.

Finding a Plant Ally

Find a plant ally. The first step in this quest is to ask. When you're meditating in that special place you've chosen, ask the spirits of the place to help you find a plant that is willing to work with you as an ally, an intermediary with the green realm. "Plant" in this context means a particular species, not an individual plant.

It should be one that grows in your eco-region, either wild or in gardens. Yes, it could be a tree, but for this exercise I'm going to suggest requesting an herb, vegetable, wildflower, or small bush, like rose or blueberry. Something may come to mind immediately—maybe rosemary, or honeysuckle, or prickly pear. If it's not obvious to you right away, that's OK. Just pay attention over the next few days and see what plants are brought to your attention.

You may see the actual plant growing somewhere. You might see an article about it in the gardening section of your local paper. You may go to a restaurant and remember how much you love an herb that's been used in the dish you ordered. When I was first doing a similar exercise many years ago, I needed shampoo, found a nice rosemary shampoo at the store, and remembered how much I love rosemary.

This isn't a major decision like choosing a spouse or a home. You'll have more than one plant ally. Maybe lots more. Some will be with you for a specific period of time, others will be with you for the rest of your life. So don't get all caught up in whether or not you are choosing the "right" one. Watch the synchronicities, and if more than one comes to your attention, just pick one. You can work with the others later.

Now that you have your plant, it's time to get to know it. I usually get all the intellectual stuff out of the way first, so my rational "science mind" will have some information to chew on. Otherwise, when I sit down to meditate, it's going to be haranguing me with questions like, "But what's its planting zone? What other plants are in the genus? Does it need full sun? Will it grow in the sandy loam soil of my backyard? Is it native to my bio region? If so, what's its niche? If not, is it invasive? How did it get here? Where else in the world does it grow? What do its flowers and seeds look like? What eats it? What pH does it prefer? Is it used as food or medicine, and if so, how?"

You may prefer to do the intuitive, meditative work with it first, then see if your intuitive perceptions matched up with what is known about it, researching answers to questions like the ones above. The internet should have most of the information you need—you're not writing a thesis or dissertation, just getting to know your new friend.

You'll also want to get to know the overlighting spirit of the plant. You'll find that each type of plant has its own overlighting spirit with which you can communicate. There are several ways of accomplishing this.

To begin, this would involve simply finding the plant in nature or acquiring some part of it—dried leaves, flowers, or root—and sitting with it in meditation—preferably at your spot out in Nature, but your altar will do. Let your mind focus on the plant, gently. Let your thoughts roam a bit as long as their primary focus is the plant. Tell the plant you would like to get to know it better, if it is willing, then see where your mind goes, what thoughts pop up that seem pertinent. This is not about hearing voices in your head. You're turning the dial, finding the best reception. There will be some static—the plant isn't trying to remind you to get cat food on your way home (that's your cat!), so when your thoughts travel that far afield, bring them back to the plant.

Notice what thoughts arise as you contemplate the plant. You're not looking for actual communication this first time, just mutual awareness. And some of you might want to leave it at that. But if you keep going with this type of meditation over the weeks and months, eventually you'll both tune in and you will pick up thoughts that seem to come from the plant. If that bothers you, you can just keep your meditations on a level of mutual awareness. The plant's not going to invade your head. But if you'd like to take the communication much further, you'll need to learn about various types of trancework. Trancework is one way we'll kiss the sky this month, but before we go there, there's one more thing you might want to do to touch the earth.

Working with Plants

Make an herbal tincture, a loose incense (the kind you burn on charcoal), or some kind of herbal personal-care product. I'm not going to go into the how-to of that here, but I've listed several good books on herbalism and making incense in the resources section of this chapter. If you are drawn to working more with plants, they will give you the guidance you need. I probably don't need to tell you that it might be a good idea to use your plant ally in these endeavors.

⊣ KISS THE SKY ⊢

Learn about Trance

Study trance states. Trance is basic to any spiritual work that goes beyond rote physical observances, such as going to church, or simple intellectual theorizing, or basic meditation. It takes different forms in different religious and spiritual traditions, but if you want to expand your awareness into the realm of spirit, then you'll need to expand your mind.

Some people call what they do shamanic journey or pathworking, meditation, or trance, and all of these things can have different methodologies and underlying philosophies, but they all lead you to a wider awareness of the ground of being, to the underlying love and creativity of Consciousness. A trance state allows our minds to tune themselves to different realities, to different forms of Consciousness, by taking our immediate attention off of our physical surroundings and directing in inward.

You'll want to start your studies now because by the time we get to Samhain, or autumn midpoint, it would be helpful if you were able to achieve a trance state for some of the work we'll do then.

Learn about Plants

Read some books on herbalism and/or local plant ecology, and/or botany. Back when I was in grad school, I had a t-shirt that read "Chlorophyll Power!" illustrated by a raised fist coming out of the ground clutching a bean seedling. (Activists were all about raised fists back then.) I admit I've always been something of an activist for plants, but you should be too! After all, they really are not only at the base of our food supply but the entire ecology of our planet. We should all know something about them.

Expand Your Imagination

Read at least one fantasy or science fiction book. Preferably two or three from the list below. Good fiction exercises and expands your imagination, which will help with your magical practice. This spiritual journey you are taking demands a strong, creative imagination.

Resources

Deborah Blake, *Midsummer: Rituals, Recipes & Lore for Litha* (St. Paul: Llewellyn Publications, 2015).

Plant Allies

Stephen Harrod Buhner, *The Secret Teachings of Plants: The Intelligence of the Heart in the Direct Perception of Nature* (Rochester: Bear and Company, 2004).

Christopher Penczak, *The Plant Spirit Familiar* (Salem: Copper Cauldron Publishing, 2011).

Machaelle Small Wright, *Perelandra Garden Workbook: A Complete Guide to Gardening with Nature Intelligences* (Warrenton: Perelandra Ltd., 1993).

The Findhorn Community, *The Findhorn Garden Story: Inspired Color Photos Reveal the Magic* (Forres: Findhorn Press, 2012).

Pam Montgomery, *Plant Spirit Healing: A Guide to Working with Plant Consciousness* (Rochester: Bear & Company, 2008).

Botany and Ecology

Brian Capon, *Botany for Gardeners* (Portland: Timber Press, 2010).

Joseph Smillie and Grace Gershun, *The Soul of Soil* (Chelsea: Chelsea Green, 1999).

Michael Pollan, *The Botany of Desire: A Plant's-Eye View of the World* (New York: Random House, 2001).

David George Haskell, *The Forest Unseen: A Year's Watch in Nature* (New York: Penguin Books, 2012).

Annie Dillard, *Pilgrim at Tinker Creek* (New York: Harper Perennial, 2013).

Herbs and Incense

Rosemary Gladstar, *Rosemary Gladstar's Herbal Recipes for Vibrant Health* (North Adams: Storey Publishing, 2015).

Scott Cunningham, *The Complete Book of Incense, Oils and Brews* (St. Paul: Llewellyn Publications, 2009).

Arin Murphy-Hiscock, *The Green Witch: Your Complete Guide to the Natural Magic of Herbs, Flowers, Essential Oils, and More* (Mills River: Adams Media, 2017).

Carl F. Neal, *Incense: Crafting & Use of Magickal Scents* (St. Paul: Llewellyn Publications, 2003).

Trance and Shamanism

Janet Farrar and Gavin Bone, *Lifting the Veil: A Witches' Guide to Trance-Prophesy, Drawing Down the Moon, and Ecstatic Ritual* (Portland: Acorn Guild Press, 2016).

Sandra Ingerman and Hank Wesselman, *Awakening to the Spirit World: The Shamanic Path of Direct Revelation* (Boulder: Sounds True, 2010).

Diana Paxson, *Trance-portation: Learning to Navigate the Inner World* (Newburyport: Weiser Books, 2008).

Sandra Ingerman, *Shamanic Journeying: A Beginner's Guide* (Boulder: Sounds True, 2008).

Fantasy/SciFi

Kenneth Grahame, *The Wind in the Willows* (Bristol: Pook Press, 2016).

J. R. R. Tolkien, *The Hobbit* and *The Lord of the Rings* (New York: Harper Collins, 2017).

Emma Bull, *War for the Oaks* (New York: Ace Books, 1987).

Marion Z. Bradley, *Mists of Avalon* (New York: Del Rey, 1984).

Janet Morris, *Dream Dancer (Kerrion Empire Book 1)* (New York: Harper Collins, 1980).

And pretty much anything by Charles de Lint, Ursula LeGuin, Terry Pratchett, Robin Hobb, Robert Silverberg, Katherine Kerr, Elizabeth Moon, Patricia Briggs, Neil Gaiman, Liz Williams, J. K. Rowling, Patrick Rothfuss, Brandon Sanderson, Patricia McKillip, Guy Gavriel Kay, and a whole host of other fine authors you'll discover as you go along. These are just some of my favorites.

CHAPTER THIRTEEN
Connecting with the Land

We've looked at gods and spirits, connected with plants, and considered what spirits may inhabit our local landbase. But the essence of an Earth-based spirituality is a larger encompassing view of the land and our connection to it. We need to look at the bigger picture.

A stronger connection with the land, the spirits of the land, and the intricate web of life upon it offers us not only a better, saner, healthier way of living, but a deep well of magic from which we can draw as we create our lives.

The Elements

Let's look at the natural world from the biggest perspective possible, the metaphysical building blocks of matter, the four classical elements. This conceptual pattern of how reality is structured has been around since the days of Plato and fully informs astrology and most Western magical traditions. These are obviously not the one hundred-plus elements which make up the periodic table that is plastered on the walls of every high school science lab. But take your mind back to your high school or college chemistry class and recall the four states of matter—gas (Air), plasma (Fire), liquid (Water), and solid (Earth). If something exists, it must be in one of these four states. The elements are foundational to our reality.

Learning how to work consciously with the elements is one of the first things you'll encounter in most magical training programs, and if you choose to pursue this training yourself, you'll find that Nature begins to respond to your expanded awareness or connection in some very magical ways. For instance, when an experienced ritualist is calling the elements into a circle outdoors, a breeze may spring up when they call Air and candles or bonfires may flare as Fire is called.

I realize this idea of Nature responding directly to you in this way can be hard to believe and may seem like the most extreme kind of solipsism. The way I think of it is that we all emit a personalized vibration that interacts with every being and every thing nearby in the same way that sound waves travel through the air. It's not that we "create" a breeze or "make" the fire jump, but if those things are in the realm of the possible at the time we are shifting our own vibration into alignment with them, then there can be a direct response to our personal vibrational shifts and changes.

Here's an example from my own life. Many years ago, some friends and I rented a beach house for a week on the Outer Banks of North Carolina. One of the interesting things about the beach there was that you could walk out into the water a very long way before the water got above your chest. Eventually, it dropped off rather suddenly into deep ocean.

One of these friends was someone who had trained with me in the first coven I was part of, and one day she and I wandered down to the beach and out into the water. As we were walking further and further out, we began talking about our studies of and experiences with the elements during those first years and how our training had made us feel so much more connected to the natural world. We spoke of how we could tune in to the consciousness of Nature—the joy of a sprouting seed, the determined power of a storm—and of how much we loved and felt connected to the creative, Moon-ruled tides of the ocean we were wading through and, through it, the element of Water.

By now, the water was up to our chests and we slowed down. We could see we weren't far from the drop-off where the water changed color. As I looked ahead, I shot out my arm to stop my friend. She froze as she saw the fin I was looking at not more than twenty feet in front of us. But then, before we could take even one step back, three or four dolphins leapt into the air, much to our delight, and continued to frolic and play for several minutes as we laughed and exclaimed at their antics. We were close enough to make eye connection once or twice, and it felt to both of us like they knew we were there.

Finally, with a flip of their tails, they dove deeply and swam away, leaving us feeling blessed, stunned, and laughing. Neither of us doubted that this was a response to the vibes we had sent out as we spoke to each other of the sacred relationship we felt with the ocean. It's not that we drew the dolphins to us but that they sensed we were there, sensed our "feeling-tone," and responded from their own well of joy and sense of camaraderie.

Might it have been pure coincidence? Sure, it could have been. But when these kinds of "coincidences" keep happening on a regular basis and your own perception repeatedly tells you that you are connecting with another intelligent being, then coincidence begins to seem like a very weak brew.

No, we can't explain these kinds of occurrences on a scientific level (yet), but we also cannot discount our own experiences. Ignoring actual experience is about as unscientific as you can get. It is also unscientific to say that something cannot be because we can't figure out how it might work. We don't need to understand the mechanism of how something works to consider whether or not it actually does exist.

A lot of people have experiences of communing with nonphysical consciousnesses, and for all the disparaging of anecdotal evidence, if there is a lot of it, then it's quite likely something's going on. Maybe it's mass hallucination, or wishful thinking, or something we don't know much about yet. That means it's time for research that can help separate the signal from the noise.

But as you consider the possibilities on an intellectual level, I urge you to begin engaging the elements in meditation and ritual, both as states of matter and states of consciousness. I capitalize the names of the elements because, as you'll discover if you take your studies further, they are conscious beings. While we can't really grasp the totality of such a being, there are what some witches and magicians refer to as "Guardians" of these elements—spirits whose level of consciousness is closer to our own and so can communicate with us. There are types of nature spirits associated with each element that are also accessible to those of us who recognize them.

But the elements are beings who encompass and hold a entire resonance of manifestation of Consciousness into material reality. The elements are very large consciousnesses, and in many ways very foreign from our own.

You may have already run across ways of working with the elements in your reading. If not, check out one of the books in the references section of this chapter. Understanding and working with the elements is a very empowering form of magic.

Before I move on, I want to note that some systems of metaphysics and healing use other elemental patterns. Traditional Chinese medicine and Taoism, for instance, use a five-element system of Wood, Fire, Earth, Metal, and Water. The Dagara tribe of West Africa works with Fire, Water, Earth, Mineral, and Nature. You might want to explore these or other ways of approaching the elements. Though I've studied several, I always return to the system that maps so well to the phases of matter because it makes the most sense to me. But I suggest that you study at least one elemental system in depth because they are basic to a metaphysical understanding of the patterns of our world.

Nature Spirits

In chapter 11, we considered the possibility of every tree, every stream, every blade of grass being conscious. We considered that Consciousness not only pervades every atom and molecule of physical reality but takes many different forms. Some of those forms are not at all related to our physical world; some have physical existences that are in dimensions not open to us; and some have the kind of consciousness that can bridge different dimensions. Gods, for instance, have agency within our physical realm but rarely exist within it as we do. Even if they manifest in human form, they don't forget who they are.

So let's expand our exploration of Consciousness into some of the larger beings with which we share our planet—spirits of Nature whose consciousness can entwine with and encompass many other consciousnesses. A forest, for example, will have an overlighting consciousness that encompasses not only trees but the understory plants, the animals, the water that flows through it, and the fungi, insects, and soil microbes that are essential to the overall functioning of the ecosystem. These types of spirits are called *genius loci*, an ancient Roman term referring to the guardian spirit of a place.

Keep in mind that we have, as yet, a very minimal understanding of the way Consciousness organizes itself. We don't know what the smallest unit of Consciousness is (assuming the concept of "unit" even holds outside of our own space/time reality). Since Consciousness is, quite literally, All That Is, the range of possibilities of types of individual consciousnesses is huge.

Because we don't have an external physical form to interact with when it comes to beings of spirit, it can be difficult to ascertain if we are, in fact, interacting with the same spirit when we discuss our experiences with, say, the spirit of Lake Erie, or the overlighting spirit of dolphins or bears. This makes it difficult to be objective and scientific about the reality of these beings, but that is the way of relationship. Two people can be discussing a third person and have such radically different experiences of that person that it can seem they are discussing two entirely different people.

As you move ahead with getting to know some of these beings, you may find that your experience of Bear, for example, does not necessarily align with someone else's experiences of Bear. Maybe you are getting entirely different information from that being or have an entirely different emotional response to it than your friend, or the author of some book or article about Bear. That's OK. There are a few possible reasons for this.

1. You could simply be wrong. You have either not made contact with the spirit of Bear or you are misunderstanding their communications. Practice makes perfect, so keep working on improving communication. Just don't make any life-altering decisions based on information that you aren't sure is from a trustworthy source.

2. You may be using the same name for different spirits. Names are fluid things. If you question the spirits a little further you may find, for instance, that you are communicating with the overlighting spirit of Black Bear, while the friend who had such a different experience is in contact with Grizzly Bear, or the prehistoric Cave Bear.

3. You may simply have a very different relationship with the same being.

No matter the reason, the answer is the same—keep working on refining your communication while checking in regularly with the results of that communication in physical reality. We'll discuss how to do that in the next chapter.

Before we move on, let me address some language issues. First, the Sanskrit word *deva* is frequently used to refer to nature spirits. Back in the late nineteenth and early twentieth centuries, the Theosophists got hold of the word and it has been carried through into various strains of occultism and New Age thought. Translated from the Sanskrit (the ancient language of India, and the scriptural language of Hinduism) it means simply "deity" or "being of light."

It's a lovely word, and there are several reasons I rarely use it. First, "nature spirit" is not an accurate translation. Also, the term is used in Buddhism, Hinduism, and Jainism to mean different things. Finally, it is also a masculine gendered term in Sanskrit. The feminine term is *devi*. I'm going to avoid it, but I want you to know what it means because you'll see it used in a some of the books in the resources section of this chapter. Other words you may come across for the realms of spirit beings are the "Otherworld(s)," or "non-ordinary reality."

The Fae and the Faery Realm

There is another group of spirits who are intertwined with the life of the planet, particularly tied with the plants and animals. They seem to have the ability to appear in our reality but have their primary existence in another dimension that is nonetheless tightly tied to this planet and our dimension. Yes, I mean faeries, or fairies, but we're not talking about Tinkerbell here. The Fae are not the tiny winged beings of pop culture, though pop culture created Tinkerbell and her ilk from the legends of the Fae.

Remember the earlier discussion of etheric bodies? How our physical body is patterned on energetic blueprints of increasing density? Well, the planet has its own energetic blueprints, and my experience of the Faery Realm is that it exists in something like an "etheric body" of the planet, an energetic dimension that helps shape our world. The Fae, to my understanding, are a critical part of the physical manifestation of Nature and the Web of Life.

What we know as the Fae are primarily associated with the Celtic lands and myths. But there are similar beings in most cultures, such as the Nunnehi of the Cherokee, and the Kontomblé of the Dagara.

They are beings of power, and the myths and traditional ways of interacting with them vary. I caution you to approach them with respect, if you choose to approach them at all. You may not. That's fine. But if you do, I strongly suggest reading several of the books listed below before you do much beyond leaving offerings.

Working Magically with the Land

Since the early days of the Industrial Revolution, poets among us have mourned the death of our rich connection with the natural world. Way back in 1807, William Wordsworth wrote:

> The world is too much with us; late and soon,
> Getting and spending, we lay waste our powers;—
> Little we see in Nature that is ours;
> We have given our hearts away, a sordid boon!
> This Sea that bares her bosom to the Moon;
> The winds that will be howling at all hours,
> And are up-gathered now like sleeping flowers;
> For this, for everything, we are out of tune;
> It moves us not. Great God! I'd rather be
> A Pagan suckled in a creed outworn;
> So might I, standing on this pleasant lea,
> Have glimpses that would make me less forlorn;
> Have sight of Proteus rising from the sea;
> Or hear old Triton blow his wreathèd horn.[14]

But, as it turns out, our Pagan creed is not outworn—it is, in fact, alive and well within the land. But we must get back in tune by reclaiming our hearts, reclaiming our power, and reconnecting with the spirits that underlie the natural world.

Once you have come to know the elements, nature spirits, and (perhaps) the Fae, you will find that you have come into a level of resonance with the land that is palpable. Resonance is a key to this kind of magic—resonance with the elements, with spirits, with the land itself—along with emotion and a strong, focused mind. There are many different ways of magically working with the land—the books listed below will give you a start. But the first thing to do is get to know it. We'll work on that at Lammas, the summer/autumn midpoint.

---

14. William Wordsworth, *Poems in Two Volumes* (London: Longman, Hurst, Rees, and Orms, 1807).

Resources

Elements

Sorita d'Este, *Practical Elemental Magick: A Guide to the Four Elements (Air, Fire, Water & Earth) in the Western Esoteric Tradition* (London: Avalonia Books, 2008).

Deborah Lipp, *The Way of Four: Create Elemental Balance in Your Life* (St. Paul: Llewellyn Publications, 2004).

Gede Parma and Jane Meredith, *Elements of Magic: Reclaiming Earth, Air, Fire, Water & Spirit* (St. Paul: Llewellyn Publications, 2018).

Mantak Chia, *Fusion of the Five Elements: Meditations for Transforming Negative Emotions* (Merrimac: Destiny Books, 2007).

Tenzin Wangyal Rinpoche and Mark Dahlby, *Healing with Form, Energy, and Light: The Five Elements in Tibetan Shamanism, Tantra, and Dzogchen* (Boulder: Snow Lion, 2002).

Fae

John Matthews, *The Sidhe: Wisdom from the Celtic Otherworld* (Traverse City: Lorian Press, 2011).

Eddie Lenihan and Carolyn Eve Green, *Meeting the Other Crowd: The Fairy Stories of Hidden Ireland* (New York: TarcherPerigee, 2004).

David Spangler, *Conversations with the Sidhe* (Traverse City: Lorian Press, 2014).

Orion Foxwood, *The Tree of Enchantment: Ancient Wisdom and Magic Practices of the Faery Tradition* (Newburyport: Weiser Books, 2008).

R.J. Stewart, *The Well of Light: From Faery Healing to Earth Healing* (Berkeley Springs: R.J. Stewart Books, 2007).

Emily Carding, *Faery Craft: Weaving Connections with the Enchanted Realm* (St. Paul: Llewellyn Publications, 2012).

Working with the Land

Doreen Valiente, *Natural Magic* (London: Robert Hale, 1998).

Machaelle Small Wright, *Behaving as if the God in All Life Mattered* (Jeffersonton: Perelandra, 1997).

Pauline Campanelli, *Wheel of the Year: Living the Magical Life* (St. Paul: Llewellyn Publications, 1988).

Ross Heaven and Howard G. Charing, *Plant Spirit Shamanism: Traditional Techniques for Healing the Soul* (Merrimac: Destiny Books, 2006).

Paul Hawken, *The Magic of Findhorn* (Forres: Findhorn Press, 2006).

Scott Cunningham, *Earth Power: Techniques of Natural Magic* (St. Paul: Llewellyn Publications, 2013).

Lupa, *Plant and Fungus Totems: Connect with Spirits of Field, Forest, and Garden* (St. Paul: Llewellyn Publications, 2014).

R. Ogilvie Crombie, *Encounters with Nature Spirits: Co-creating with the Elemental Kingdom* (Forres: Findhorn Press, 2018).

Sandra Ingerman, *Walking in Light: The Everyday Empowerment of a Shamanic Life* (Boulder: Sounds True, 2015).

Lammas—The Summer/ Autumn Midpoint

This midpoint between Summer Solstice and Autumn Equinox happens in the midst of the proverbial dog days of summer. Traditionally, the holiday of Lammas falls on August 1; astronomically, it happens right around August 7, in the middle of the sign of Leo. The days are clearly growing shorter, but day length is not changing as quickly as it will in the weeks to come, since the rate of change to fewer daylight hours increases as we move closer to the equinox. It is the first of three harvest festivals and celebrates the "first fruits" of the harvest. It's not as though there's no food being harvested before August, but the food that stores well, the food that gets us through the winter, is the focus now. After months of growth, we can begin to harvest and store.

Summer's heat still reigns, and the days are longer than the nights, but there is more ripening than growing happening, as Nature begins to prepare for the coming winter. Traditionally, this holiday celebrates wheat and other grains, and you'll want to consider which grains are ripening or ripe at this time in your area. Through much of the Northern Hemisphere, wheat that is planted the previous fall is harvested in June or July. By the time August rolls around in a non-mechanized agricultural system, there would have been time to dry, thresh, and grind the wheat into flour, making early August a fine time to celebrate the new crop with lots of bread. In the more northern areas, a spring-planted wheat is generally grown, which ripens in August, making early August a fine time to use up what remains of last year's flour by baking lots of bread.

This focus on bread is reflected in one of the traditional names for this holiday, Lammas, a word derived from the Anglo-Saxon *hlaf-mas*, translated as "loaf mass" ("mass" referring to the religious ceremony). Other names are Lughnasadh and Lunasa, both referring to the Irish god Lugh, a warrior god who honors skill, craft, and the arts. Lughnasadh was, of old, a celebration that incorporated games of skill and the display of crafts in honor of Lugh's foster mother, Tailtiu. Lúnasa is another spelling for the holiday, and also Modern Irish for the month of August.

The overall theme for this holiday is one of celebration—of the harvest, and of our human skills and crafts, particularly the agricultural and practical ones, such as pottery and blacksmithing. There are always state, county, and other agricultural fairs and festivals going on around this time, and they do a fine job of showcasing local talent and celebrating the first fruits of the harvest.

─┤ TOUCH THE EARTH ├─

Caring for the Land

As always, one of the first things to do at any of our way stations on the Wheel of the Year is note where Sun rises and sets and spend some time out in Nature, observing. Now that you have your place in Nature where you can go to meditate and connect with Earth and the Web of Life, you have one spot from which you can carefully observe seasonal changes.

Before you go there to celebrate this turning of the Wheel of the Year, think about what service you might do for the land and its creatures. Is there trash that needs to be picked up? Is there a type of plant native to your area that is struggling in the face of invasives and habitat destruction but would grow well and fit right in to the ecology of your little spot? Perhaps you could purchase some seeds or seedlings and find a good place for them to grow. (You should only use plants you are certain are not just native to the local ecosystem but also going to the right spot within that ecosystem. If you have any doubts at all, don't do this.) Or it could be that you need to get involved politically to restrain local development and further habitat destruction.

If you aren't sure what to do, tune in to the spirits of the place when you go there and ask for guidance. As always, it may not come to you right away, but pay attention over the next couple of weeks for synchronicities that lead you to an understanding of how you can help heal and/or protect that area of land you've chosen to connect with.

From now on, you'll want to bring an offering to your special place on all eight of the holidays, but especially this one. Cornmeal will do quite well, but so would offerings of "first fruits" from actual fruit to honey or whole grains. Just keep in mind that fruit contains and grains are seeds, and you don't want to sow anything that is not native to the ecosystem. Things you've prepared yourself from the harvest, like cornbread, fruit jam, herb vinegar, applesauce, pickles, or homemade cherry brandy are an ideal offering and will not have fertile seeds. Just make sure to leave small amounts that will be eaten or decompose quickly. More is not better. Just like a tiny USB drive can carry terabytes of data, so can a teaspoon of cornmeal and an ounce of water carry a full charge of gratitude and intention.

Create from the Harvest

Make some kind of herbal extract, incense, or special food, like those mentioned above, from a local harvest. A trip to the farmers' market or your own garden will tell you what's in season. See what draws you, buy some, and do something with it. There are plenty of recipes online, but the one thing you don't want to forget is to add some magic to your recipe. There are lots of ways to do this.

You can simply hold each of the ingredients between your two hands, giving thanks and speaking a blessing over each of the ingredients as you put something together in your kitchen. Or you can sit at your altar, light some candles and incense, and meditate deeply on whatever intention you want to imbue your creation with while holding either the ingredients or the finished product between your hands and directing the energy of your intention into it.

Cooking Magically

Find at least one way to bring more magic into your kitchen and food preparation. For instance, get a special glass-enclosed candle (I use red, the color of life). Hold it, go into a meditative state, and imbue it with your intentions for the food you prepare—health, joy, love, and pleasure. Then light it when you cook. There are other suggestions in some of the books below, but whatever you do, when you cook, stay aware of the magic that is happening.

Cook something special. Bread is good, but anything that uses recently harvested local ingredients is fine. If you are gluten-free, there are still lots of options for special treats. (Gluten-free blueberry clafoutis! Yum!) Whatever you make, it should be cooked, not just a bowl of fruit or salad. Cooking is a magical act of transformation in itself—an interaction of the elements, driven by Fire—which makes it easier for the cook to imbue the food with their magical intentions and blessings.

Share it with family or friends—maybe in a ritual setting or just over dinner or dessert. You might consider discussing what you are each grateful for in your lives or the skills you would like to improve over the next year.

Off to the Fair

Go to an agricultural fair! Visit a state fair or county fair and get to know what food is grown and raised in your area. Thank a farmer while you're there—providing food is a lot of work.

⊣ KISS THE SKY ⊢

Our mental focus during this season will be on connecting with some of the larger consciousnesses of Nature, starting with a tree, then journaling about the experiences and how they have affected our beliefs.

Certainly, many of us who work on developing what I'll call "extended senses"—the ability to see/hear/sense energy that bridges the physical and nonphysical—are well aware that it is not only humans who radiate subtle energy fields. Animals, plants, trees, and the planet itself all have subtle energy templates, and it is through these fields that most of us begin to communicate with non-human forms of life and consciousness. As we work on expanding our awareness of Earth and its inhabitants, we'll use this form of communication a lot. Here's an exercise to start you off that will help you develop your extended senses, and also help you ground and balance your own energy.

Connecting with a Tree

Find a tree where you can sit or stand with your back against it. For some of you, this might be difficult—city dwellers will probably need to go to a park. Your best bet is a fairly isolated area where you won't be disturbed, but safety may be an issue. You'll be working with your eyes closed and your attention elsewhere, so you may want to bring a friend as a lookout for you. And, of course, there are certain ecosystems that are treeless. If you live in one of them, then choose a plant that is long-lived and influential on the ecosystem. Saguaro cactus, for instance, would be appropriate if you live in a desert ecosystem where the saguaro grows.

Put your hands on the tree. (If it's a cactus, just get as close as you can. Putting your hands on the ground close to the base should be sufficient.) Close your eyes and ask the tree if it would be willing to work with you, to share its awareness. Most of you will probably think, "But how will I *know* what the answer is?" You won't. Not in the sure-and-certain way that you want, like talking to an Ent in *The Lord of the Rings* movies. Go with your gut instinct, but first, check in with your ego. Be self-aware enough to become aware of any ego-based desires ("This is such a big, beautiful old oak; I want to say it's *my* tree and tell people that *I* can talk to it!"). See those desires for what they are and look beyond them. Tune in to your body—it may tell you more about what the tree is communicating to you than your mind. Once you've done that, though, just make your best decision and don't second-guess yourself.

Leaning your back against the tree or sitting close to your cactus with your back toward it and your spine straight, close your eyes and focus on your breathing. Breathe into your belly first, then bring it up like a wave into your chest. Reverse as you exhale. Once you've taken a few deep breaths, let your breath normalize but check to make sure you are breathing into your belly.

Let yourself become aware of what you can hear, smell, and feel around you. Be in the present moment. Feel the solidity of the tree against your back. Is there a breeze? Can you sense the wind through the branches? Feel the solid earth under you.

Now extend your mind and senses into the tree and see if you can feel the motion of energy within the tree itself. Here's how it works in the physical realm: During the day, in a season when the tree has leaves, those leaves take in carbon dioxide from the air and light from the Sun and use them to form sugars through the process of photosynthesis. This process also requires water and certain minerals, and the roots take those things in and send them up to the leaves through special tubes, called the xylem, that permeate the tree. In return, the leaves send dissolved sugars back to the roots through other tubes called phloem, and the roots use those sugars as food so they can grow further. Meanwhile, the leaves are excreting oxygen, which is a byproduct of photosynthesis, and other gases.

In the winter, of course, the flow will be extremely slow or nonexistent, though the sap is still in the tree (it does not sink into the roots, as folklore would have it), which is why it's best to do this exercise when there are green leaves on the tree, at least at first. Choose a warmish, sunny day.

See if you can sense this reciprocal flow of water and minerals up to the leaves and sugars down to the roots as the tree inhales carbon dioxide and exhales oxygen. Go ahead and just imagine at first. Then pay attention and, at some point, you'll feel a shift in your awareness when that connection is made between the imaginal realm and reality, and you become aware of the tree on another level. As astrologer Caroline Casey often notes, "Imagination lays the tracks for the reality train to follow."

The level you're connecting on is the level of your subtle body and the tree's. Sense how your own energy body has merged with the tree's. Imagine a flow of Earth (as dissolved minerals) and Water coming up into your body through your spine, and a flow of Air and Fire (sunlight) diffusing into your body through your skin, or just imagine that you have roots drawing up earth and water, and leaves that are absorbing sunlight and exchanging carbon dioxide and oxygen into the surrounding air.

Let the energy of these elements flow through you, allowing them to come to balance within your body for your perfect health. Earth strengthens your bones and provides the minerals your cells need to build their various structures. Water cleanses your cells of waste and creates the blood and fluids that keep your body functioning. Air brings the exchange of gases through lungs and skin, fueling the Fire that is our metabolism—the spark of life within us.

Once you feel balanced, spend some time communing with the tree, letting it show you a different way of being than your human one. Try to determine what the tree might need that you could offer it. Let yourself feel gratitude for the tree's presence in your life and its place in the local ecosystem. When you feel that your conversation is complete for the day, thank the tree and detach your awareness from the tree slowly as you bring your focus back to your body and breath. Open your eyes when you're ready. Step away from the tree, do some grounding and centering, sense yourself as fully separate from the tree, then leave water and cornmeal or some other appropriate offering for the tree.

If you keep practicing like this, you'll find that as your ability to tune in to the tree improves, its awareness will help you tune in to your own body and direct these subtle energies, and your health will improve as well. Working with a tree is a great way to begin to sense the energies that connect us to the Web of Life and to the planet itself.

Connect with a Genius Loci

This exercise should be done only after you have made a connection with your tree (or cactus, or whatever). There are several reasons for this, but essentially, the tree can introduce you to the genius loci, or overlighting protective spirit of the area. As in everyday life, introductions are helpful so you know to whom you are speaking.

To do this, repeat the exercise above until you feel connected with the tree. Then ask the tree if it is willing to help facilitate your connection with the genius loci of this place. If you get a no, ask if you should try at a different time or if you need to find another tree. When you get a yes, then mentally send out a request to meet the genius loci of this place. Let the tree amplify your request and send it out on the right frequency. Then just quiet your mind and note what you sense/hear/intuit.

You may or may not make a connection this first time. If you do, then introduce yourself! Tell this spirit that you are working to strengthen your connection with the natural world. Ask what you can do to help to balance and strengthen the local ecosystem. Eventually, this connection will lead you to a deep sense of connection and a well of magical power you can draw on, but start off right—offer a gift and establish a relationship before asking for a favor.

As always, be aware that you can refuse any spirit's request and ask them to explain themselves or their actions, and they cannot make you do anything you don't want to do. Again, keeping a journal of your experiences will help you learn, as will reading some of the books in this resources section.

Resources

Lammas

Melanie Marquis, *Lughnasadh: Rituals, Recipes & Lore for Lammas* (St. Paul: Llewellyn Publications, 2015).

Cooking and Herbalism

Mary Mason Campbell, *The New England Butt'ry Shelf Cookbook: Receipts for Very Special Occasions* (Brattleboro: Stephen Greene Press, 1982).

Scott Cunningham, *The Complete Book of Incense, Oils and Brews* (St. Paul: Llewellyn Publications, 2009).

Rosalee de la Forêt, *Alchemy of Herbs: Transform Everyday Ingredients into Foods and Remedies That Heal* (Carlsbad: Hay House, 2017).

Spencre L. R. McGowan, *Blotto Botany: A Lesson in Healing Cordials and Plant Magic* (New York: Morrow Gift, 2018).

Maia Toll, *The Illustrated Herbiary: Guidance and Rituals from 36 Bewitching Botanicals* (North Adams: Storey Publishing, 2018).

Rosemary Gladstar, *Rosemary Gladstar's Herbal Recipes for Vibrant Health: 175 Teas, Tonics, Oils, Salves, Tinctures, and Other Natural Remedies for the Entire Family* (Carlsbad: Storey Publishing, 2015).

Gail Faith Edwards, *Opening Our Wild Hearts to the Healing Herbs* (Woodstock: Ash Tree Publishing, 2000).

Connecting with Nature Spirits

Sandra Ingerman and Llyn Roberts, *Speaking with Nature: Awakening to the Deep Wisdom of the Earth* (Rochester: Bear & Company, 2015).

Robin Wall Kimmerer, *Braiding Sweetgrass: Indigenous Wisdom, Scientific Knowledge and the Teachings of Plants* (Minneapolis: Milkweed Editions, 2013).

Pam Montgomery, *Plant Spirit Healing: A Guide to Working with Plant Consciousness* (Rochester: Bear & Company, 2010).

Marko Pogacnik, *Nature Spirits & Elemental Beings: Working with the Intelligence in Nature* (Forres: Findhorn Press, 2012).

Lupa, *Nature Spirituality From the Ground Up: Connect with Totems in Your Ecosystem* (St. Paul: Llewellyn Publications, 2016).

CHAPTER FIFTEEN
Taking Psi Out for a Spin

For a lot of people, developing their own psychic abilities is where the rubber meets the road. After all, things like meditation, ritual, sensing subtle bodies, talking with spirits, past life experiences, and near-death experiences can be easily dismissed as "psychological" and "all in your head." But telepathy (communicating thoughts and ideas in ways that do not involve the five senses), clairvoyance (seeing remote images or events), precognition (foretelling future events), and psychokinesis (affecting objects through mental intention alone) all have checkable outcomes. It's often possible to determine, to one degree or another, whether telepathy, clairvoyance, precognition, and psychokinesis really happened.

When you finally understand that "psi" (an umbrella term used by researchers for all psychic abilities) is real, it can be life-changing. I remember when it really sank in for me. It wasn't a bolt of insight but a growing realization over a period of time. It was back in the mid-eighties, and I had recently been accepted as a student in the first coven I was ever in. I had a solid scientific education under my belt, and I'd been struggling with the disconnect between the scientific attitude toward anything paranormal and my increasing interest in Wicca and witchcraft, not to mention my already long-standing interest in and study of astrology.

The priestess of the coven had decided to open a small bookstore, and one day I was helping her set things up when a woman came in and asked about doing tarot readings at the store once it opened. She generally read tarot at her local pub, she said, but was looking to expand her clientele. She did a reading for me right then and there. The level of detail she picked up about my life was amazing; she went on to tell me that I would meet a man soon with whom I would have a rather intense relationship, and that he and I would eventually open a business together. She told me what he looked like and what he did for a living.

At the time, I had not the slightest intention of ever becoming a business owner, but as the year unfolded, I met this man (who fit her description of him to a T), the relationship unfolded as she had predicted, and we opened a business a year or so after we met. In the meantime, I had become a student of hers and often sat with her as she did readings in the pub. Her level of accuracy was astounding. No, she wasn't right all the time, but she was right far more often than not, and her predictions were remarkably detailed. I also learned, watching her, that the future was not carved in stone and the cards could be used not just to foretell the future but give advice on how to change it as well. And that advice always seemed to come from a more enlightened and expansive viewpoint than either the reader or the querent (a useful, if quaint, term for the person getting the reading) normally had access to.

The level of detail was far beyond what could be accounted for by coincidence. She gave precise predictions and got all the variables right so often it was astonishing. I knew that because I was there listening when people at the pub kept coming up to her and telling her, in detail, just how right she had been. Clearly, she was able to do something that gave her glimpses from outside of time and space. I realized that there had to be a reality beyond the physical. I began reading more and more about research being done on psi and finally began reconciling my scientific training with my lived experiences.

Even scientists all too often forget a basic scientific principle—you do not need to know *how* something works to know that it works. You do not need to know the mechanism for a phenomenon to know that the phenomenon exists or even to utilize it. Once you have verified that it exists, *then* you can figure out how it works. We did not, for example, need to know that charge is carried on subatomic particles in order to create a battery to store electrical energy.

My time studying with this woman convinced me beyond doubt that she was able to accurately and in detail predict the future for random people she didn't know. The cards were a tool, directed by a larger awareness. The understanding that our consciousness is not limited by time and space and that our minds can reach beyond those limits opened a whole new world for me, and I began a studying that world in depth.

Eventually, I opened a metaphysical bookstore (as predicted) and met lots of tarot readers. Many of them ended up doing readings at my store—I had a reader there every day—so I came to understand more about how and why tarot readings "worked." Reading tarot, or palms, or any other divinatory method combines both talent and skill. Like an athlete or an opera singer, good diviners have both a natural affinity for the work and have invested lots of time in developing their inborn skills to a high degree. The particular tools they used were a personal choice, and no one tool seemed to have any advantage over another. It was all about who was using the tool. I learned that what made a diviner a diviner was innate talent and acquired skill, not the cards or the shells or the crystal ball. Heading out to the nearest big-box hardware store and purchasing saws, hammers, screwdrivers, and drills will not make you a carpenter. Nor will heading to your nearest metaphysical store and buying three tarot decks, a set of runes, and a crystal ball make a diviner of you. It takes training and practice.

So when you read about the science that has been done to prove that psi is real, keep in mind that almost all the experiments have pulled the participants from the general population instead of using trained professionals. It's kind of like pulling groups of eleven random people off the street, telling them they are a football team, and expecting them to be able to play as well as the Dallas Cowboys. But *even so*, the scientific evidence for psi is robust and repeatable. Unsurprisingly, given the pool of subjects, the effects tend to be small. But they are statistically highly significant. Psi exists. The likelihood that you have a native ability you can develop further is high.

So, if you have the kind of rational mind that would appreciate being given something substantial to chew on before you venture off to develop your psychic abilities, then do some reading first from the books listed below. I suggest doing whatever reading or research (such as getting readings from good, professional readers) it takes to convince your left brain of the reality of psychic abilities. Or at least the possibility that they might exist. Because if it is constantly trying to convince you otherwise and tell you that you're going off the deep end believing this stuff, that will, unsurprisingly, strongly inhibit your ability to access your psychic self.

Learning to Drive

I've found that most, if not all, of us have these abilities, just as most of us have a voice—the ability to speak or even sing. There are lots of techniques that will help almost anyone who is willing to put in the work learn to at least carry a tune. Most of us can learn to drive or even race cars. We can also learn the skills of alert awareness, self-investigation, and a quiet mind that allow us to access our psychic selves. But regardless of the techniques used, psychic training involves, at first, just opening up to the possibilities. Second, it is about paying closer attention to your thoughts and emotions and developing the fine art of listening.

Opening to Possibilities

This means allowing yourself to act "as if" psychic abilities are real. When the phone rings, take a guess at who's calling. Pull a tarot card in the morning and use it to help you sense some event or emotional state you'll experience in the day ahead. If you are going someplace you've never been before, try to sense something about that place. It might be something specific, like the shape of a building or the color of paint on the walls, or it might mean sensing the emotional atmosphere of the meeting you are going to attend. If you or a friend has lost something, see if you can get some sense of where it is.

Opening to possibilities also means not getting discouraged. You will probably be wrong quite often until you learn how to keep your expectations/fears/beliefs from dictating the responses to the questions you pose to your psychic self. Keep at it. Like any other skill, psi requires constant practice.

Opening to possibilities also means exploring the roots of your skepticism. I'm a fan of rational skepticism—it's important for us to question the accuracy of our perceptions around the nature of reality if we want to learn how to change it. But I've found that, too often, skepticism is a front for an underlying fear rather than a realistic decision. Often, it's a fear of change—which may even be well-founded. Nonetheless, fear-driven skepticism is not rational. It is not even skepticism anymore—it's cobbled together from unconscious defense mechanisms that need to become conscious.

Check in with the reasons for your skepticism regularly. (And if you don't have any, then you should definitely work to develop some. Reality is not just what you choose to believe in the moment.) If you are truly being rational and not driven by unconscious emotions, then you should have no trouble putting aside both your skepticism and any other preconceptions you may have as you work to develop your own psychic abilities. Go ahead. See what happens. It might change your whole life.

Learning to Listen

This begins with recognizing the divergent parts of yourself that have ongoing conversations in your head.

"I do *not* want ice cream!"

"Of course you do. You deserve that sweetness! Here, let me remind you exactly what it tastes like!"

Intense ice cream memories flood your mind. You drag your thoughts back to the ritual you did a week ago.

"I have promised myself that I will take care of my body and only eat healthy food!"

"Ah, but you can't neglect your soul! Ice cream is food for the soul!"

Etcetera, etcetera.

The conversation might not be quite that clear, but the fact that you have competing thoughts and desires trying to dictate your actions as your hand hovers over the ice cream in the freezer makes it pretty clear that there are different parts that make up the whole of who you are, in the same way your body is composed of different parts and organs that function together as a whole. Those parts feed your present moment with various ideas, emotions, memories, and sensory awareness. Becoming more mindful of these components of yourself will allow you analyze and understand your unconscious drives and fears. Making those drives and fears conscious helps you sort the ones that are creative, helpful, and sensible from those that reflect childhood fears and emotional imprintings that range from simply limiting to downright toxic. Making them conscious allows you free yourself from self-imposed restrictions that you may not have even been aware of.

Once you have learned to listen, there are voices—maybe only one, maybe more—that you will come to recognize and wiser and more loving than most of the others. When you do become aware of those voices, try to get a sense of what it feels like when you are connecting to that part of yourself. There will be an emotional tone to the contact and often certain physical sensations as well. Once you have that discernment, you can focus your awareness on listening with more attention to the voices that encourage you, that give you good advice and reflect your core values. You may find these voices speak to you through your body as well as your mind, and learning to listen to your body's reactions can indicate to you whether or not you are in touch with your Greater Self, your guides, or any helping spirits you work with. It is from these voices you will gain psychic insights.

Meditation helps with all these things. The thought-tracking exercise I gave in chapter 6 will be a big help with this work. And as with any other skill, there will be some who have considerable natural talent and those who will struggle to develop what small ability they have. But even if you don't believe you have much ability at all, I urge you to spend at least a year working in a focused way on developing these abilities.

Developing my psychic abilities changed my life. It gave me greater insight into myself, into others, and into the nature of reality. If you work at it, you'll find your life changing for the better as well.

Resources

Ivo Dominguez, Jr., *Keys To Perception: A Practical Guide To Psychic Development* (Newburyport: Weiser Books, 2017).

Mat Auryn, *Psychic Witch: A Metaphysical Guide to Meditation, Magick & Manifestation* (St. Paul: Llewellyn Publications, 2020).

Russell Targ, *The Reality of ESP: A Physicist's Proof of Psychic Abilities* (Wheaton: Quest Books, 2012).

Chris Carter, *Science and Psychic Phenomena: The Fall of the House of Skeptics* (Rochester: Inner Traditions, 2012).

Melanie Barnum, *Llewellyn's Little Book of Psychic Development* (St. Paul: Llewellyn Publications, 2017).

Dean Radin, Ph.D., *The Conscious Universe: The Scientific Truth of Psychic Phenomena* (New York: HarperOne, 1997).

Dean Radin, Ph.D., *Entangled Minds: Extrasensory Experiences in a Quantum Reality* (New York: Paraview Pocket Books, 2006).

Lynne McTaggart, *The Field: The Quest for the Secret Force of the Universe* (New York: Harper Perennial, 2008).

Richard Webster, *Llewellyn's Complete Book of Divination: Your Definitive Source for Learning Predictive & Prophetic Techniques* (St. Paul: Llewellyn Publications, 2017).

CHAPTER SIXTEEN
Harvest Home—The Autumn Equinox

The Autumn Equinox (a.k.a. Mabon, Harvest Home, Alban Elfed) brings us once more to a time of equal dark and light, day and night. A time of balance, but heading into darkness now instead of light. We carry a lot of baggage around darkness, both cultural and biological, and it's worth unpacking that baggage as we head into the darkest time of the year—the three months before and after the Winter Solstice.

A student of mine who hailed from the Northeast and was living in western North Carolina at the time, told me that she had always disliked winter until she started studying Wicca with me. Finally, she said, she was learning to appreciate and enjoy the dark time instead of feeling the underlying anxiety that used to plague her as the days became shorter.

She, like many people, had an instinctive aversion to the dark—which makes some evolutionary sense, given the limits of our physical vision. I imagine that in cultures that put more of an emphasis on developing extended senses there is far less fear of the dark. But that's not the culture we live in, so let's take a look at how we can change our outlook by shifting our perspective a bit.

First, we need to look at which cultural assumptions about darkness we buy into. There are lots of them, and most if not all of us were imprinted with at least a few of them as children. When we are fully caught up in a cultural assumption, we don't think about it much. It's not part of our conscious awareness but lives in the sub- and/or unconscious where it influences our perceptions and reactions. That's not a bad thing in itself—if we had to care-fully consider all our beliefs, attitudes, and values around every decision we made, we'd never get anything done.

If you Google something like "color meanings in different cultures" or "psychology of color," you'll find that black is often associated with death, evil, bad luck, and criminality. This is particularly true in Western culture. Think of phrases like "the black hats" for the bad guys, "black magic" for evil magic, "black market" for illegal markets, and the "dark web" for the part of the internet that serves as a communication hub for various criminal enter-prises. Anything you want to hide can be hidden in the darkness. There's no question that this cultural attitude also influences our ongoing problem with racism.

But there are other ways of approaching the dark. It can force us to rely on our other senses instead of our eyes. It can be a place of retreat, rest, and recuperation. It can be a space in which dreams are created and nurtured. It can be where we gather power and strength sourced from the deep uncon-scious and the Otherworlds. It is a place of communion with spirit and of deep healing. The dark is as sacred as the light, the night as blessed as the day. The dark holds all possibilities, which allows the light infinite choices about what to bring into manifestation. I think of the dark as the Cauldron of Creation.

You can't only change your intellectual beliefs if you want to welcome the dark—you must recognize, evaluate, and discard at least some of the emotionally-imprinted cultural beliefs you still carry, while adopting oth-ers that are healthier and more in line with your core values. Watch your thoughts and feelings as they arise and check them against reality. This espe-cially applies to fearful thoughts and feelings.

I find the symbol of the yin-yang to be a useful one to keep in mind at the equinoxes. One curved section is black, one white. They are of equal size, and each has a seed of the other color in its center. There are other meaning-ful symbols for balance, of course. Think about what symbols draw you in, which ones speak to you and seem to resonate with meaning that you can't put into words. Those are the symbols you'll want to use for your magic and meditations.

Gratitude

The Autumn Equinox is also the time of the harvest when, in pre-industrial society, the upcoming winter either seemed secure—or not. If the harvest was poor, people would die. Death from starvation combined with cold threatened an entire community. A generous harvest meant life and was reason to give thanks to whatever deities or universal forces you felt were responsible for this gift of sufficient food.

I know quite a few people who get their backs up about the whole idea of gratitude. I used to feel that way myself. As children, we heard too much "You should be grateful!" or "Say thank you!" Gratitude seemed fake—something you had to do, instead of something you actually felt. "Oh, Aunt Emma, thank you so much for this lovely (*unbelievably ugly!*) sweater! I'll think (*unkindly*) of you every time I (*my parents make me*) wear it!"

It felt like a demand, and as adults we also came to see just how often that demand was directed at those who had far less than those who were doing the giving. Authentic gratitude cannot be demanded, but cringing, groveling, obsequiousness, or just fake smiles certainly can be, and are, all in the name of gratitude. Bah, humbug!

Then, during a "dark night of the soul" time, I was persuaded by my guides and inner promptings to go a little deeper, to look at gratitude from a different perspective, and it precipitated some big changes for me. It turns out that gratitude (the real thing, not the fake stuff) changes not only your mindset but your personal resonance. It empowers magic and deepens spiritual connection.

It took me a while to really identify what gratitude felt like, to let it rise naturally once I'd cleared away the mental and emotional debris that was the legacy of unwanted sweaters and all the other things I'd pretended to be grateful for in my life. What I discovered is that the feeling of authentic gratitude is sweet—a feeling of openness and connectedness shot through with shining ripples of love and joy. I found that when I feel real gratitude, I am connected to the cause of this feeling and deeply appreciate its being.

At first, I really had to work at it. I had to clear away the anger and resentment that are the inevitable result of fake gratitude. Rather than demanding gratitude, I explored feelings I had around beings and things in my life, and, when I found the thread of gratitude, I followed it.

My cats helped me find gratitude. In that dark night of the soul, I challenged myself to identify what I *did* feel grateful for, and my cats were first on my list. I knew I felt love for them, but when I observed my feelings more closely, I noted that I felt a deep appreciation for their "catness," for their beauty and grace, for the purrs and cuddles, and even for the occasional gift of an uneaten but very dead mouse dropped at my feet, followed by a look that said "for you" and a leap into my lap.

My new apartment helped me find gratitude. It was not given to me, I did not have to say thank you to my landlord when I paid the rent, but the fact that this apartment—perfect for me in so many ways—even existed, and that I found it, seemed like a gift. That my wonderful neighbors were my neighbors seemed like a gift, and I let myself revel in appreciation for all this goodness in my life. My inner sky began to lighten as the dark night dissipated.

I found that blossoms in spring, summer's fruits and rich greens, autumn's colorful harvest, winter's stillness, and the beauty of the bones of trees and mountains all elicited gratitude within me. So did time with my friends, a child's smile, hot soup on a cold night, and—always!—my cats. I didn't feel I had to be grateful to something or someone. I didn't feel like I owed anyone. I simply allowed my spontaneous feelings of love and appreciation to be fully experienced and shared energetically, if not verbally or physically.

I don't feel that I *have* to feel grateful for everything, and neither should you. Unless or until you've reached a level of enlightenment that is far beyond my own, there will be things in your life you are distinctly *not* grateful for —things you want to shift, or discard, or transform, or kick out of your life entirely. I've found that people who insist that they are "grateful for *everything*, even the hard stuff!" are, underneath it all, terrified that if they stop thinking positive thoughts all the damned time, their lives are going to fall apart. (And they usually do fall apart because you can't constantly repress your thoughts and emotions without real repercussions, no matter how many times you say "namaste".) But if you've read this far, you're almost certainly not that person. Just don't let anyone persuade you that you *must* be grateful for anything or everything.

I found that gratitude not only brought joy into my life, it brought joy that could be shared. It shifted my personal resonance and helped me look at life from a different perspective when I was having a tough time. It brought me into closer resonance with the magic of Nature and the elements and helped me create a better life. Now, I cultivate that feeling of gratitude. I make time to actively experience gratitude. Gratitude, I have come to find, is the precursor to feelings of wonder, awe, and connection to the universe.

Harvest Home is a fine time to cultivate gratitude. Let's look at how we can gratefully celebrate this Station of the Sun.

—| TOUCH THE EARTH |—

A Ritual for Balance

Do a ritual to balance light and dark within yourself and within your life.

Set up your altar with whatever items are basic to your altar setup, such as representations of the four elements, and the following:

- A black and a white taper candle
- A fragrant oil, perfume, or hydrosol that feels balancing to you and/or reminds you of autumn
- A symbol, such as the yin-yang, or a set of scales, that speaks to you of balance and the cycle of light and dark
- Things that represent the harvest—pumpkins, squash, apples, pears, acorns, etc. Perhaps tomatoes or peppers if you live in a warmer climate. Ideally, you'll have something in your garden or be able to go to the farmers' market and pick up something that was grown locally.
- Have your journal nearby

If you have time, take a cleansing salt bath (a cup or so of salt in a tub or bucket of water) before you begin the ritual. (If you don't have time, don't let that stop you from doing the rest of the ritual. Just wash your hands and face, and do a quick cleansing/grounding meditation.)

Sit at your altar and quiet your mind. Think about your intention for doing this ritual. It will be something like "To contemplate the balance of light and dark and bring myself in tune with the changing seasons." It's best to do this in a darkened room with just enough light so you can see where the different items are on your altar.

Take the bottle of fragrance and put some on. Breathe in the fragrance and let it awaken that feeling of autumn in you. Think about the symbol you chose and consider its meaning.

Contemplate what this season means to you personally and what it means to the ecosystem you live in. Are leaves falling? Temperatures changing? Plants dying or, in warmer climes, different plants growing? If you live near the equator, you may only notice changes in weather patterns—wind directions, storms, etc. Recall where the Sun rose at Summer Solstice and where it rises now.

Sit in the dark and consider what the darkness means to you, what part of that is nothing more than cultural baggage and what part is a natural human reaction. Think about positive aspects of darkness and the dark time of the year. Think about the interaction of dark and light, and how important it is for us to have a balance of the two—day and night, winter and summer, New and Full Moon.

Say something like this: "I stand at the balance of dark and light and welcome the darkness. I welcome the time of rest and renewal, the quiet time. I welcome the change of focus from the world of manifestation to the world of spirit. I acknowledge that, as the light contains the darkness, so the darkness contains the light."

Then say, "I welcome the light that lives within the darkness" and light your candles. Spend as much time as you want meditating, then journal about the thoughts and insights you've had. When you're done, snuff out your candles. You can relight them daily or weekly for a meditation session until they have burned away.

Working with Tarot

Get a tarot deck and use it. You don't need to do readings for yourself or anyone else, just begin to learn the meanings of the cards by pulling between one and three cards every day. Put them on your altar. See what you can pick up about the challenges and blessings of the day ahead. Make a note in your journal.

At the end of the day, reflect on what you thought the cards meant and how they were accurately reflected in the day, either in your thoughts and emotions, or in the outer world. Then look up the card in the accompanying booklet and make some more notes in your journal, paying particular attention to the symbolism on each card, not just the "meaning" of the card itself. The cards don't have single, set in stone meanings. Working with them will expand your personal symbol set.

Developing Intuition

As an exercise in developing your expanded senses, map three or four different ways to and from your workplace or some place you go regularly. Before you begin your commute, sit quietly in your car and intuit which would be the best one for you to take. You may or may not get any insight into the reason it's "the best." It may be because of traffic, or that your soul needs to see a particular vista on your way home, or for some reason you may never know. If you do this regularly, there will be little victories when you get home and realize you avoided a bad traffic jam, or you're where you need to be to help someone else, or maybe the light is shining just right through the leaves and your soul soars. For the most part, though, you can expect that you won't know why that route was best. But you'll learn to tune in to the world around you, hone your extended senses, and trust the feedback they give you.

Symbols of the Harvest

Put a cornucopia with goodies in it on your altar or dining room table as a symbolic reminder of the gifts of the harvest.

Saying Grace

Say grace at every meal. It doesn't have to be complicated. "I (we) give thanks for Earth and its blessings, for the lives that were given to nourish mine," is enough, or you can make up your own. When you cook, thank the plants and animals for their lives.

⊣ KISS THE SKY ⊢

Appreciate the Dark

As the days get shorter, we need to pay attention to how our bodies and minds are reacting to the increasing darkness. Given the shorter, colder days, many of us will not be getting enough light. Make sure to get outdoors as much as you can. But allow yourself to appreciate the dark, as well. Turn off the lights for a while. Light a candle or two. Think about what life must have been like for your ancestors, in the days before electric light. Let yourself be soothed and nourished by the darkness.

Change Your Point of View

One of the best side effects of developing intuition is that it increases empathy and compassion. Over the next month or so, make a point of consciously trying to see things from another person's point of view. Check in intuitively and/or in person with your important relationships. Are they balanced? Honest? Loving? Spend some time assessing how your relationships impact your life.

Explore Your Thoughts about the Dark

Write in your journal about darkness and your impressions of it. How many synonyms and phrases can you come up with about darkness? Examine them. Over the next few weeks, work to discard those that do not reflect your truth but the prejudices of your society. Bring new ones into your consciousness. Be persistent, and eventually you'll find that, like my student, you may find yourself looking forward to the dark time.

Develop Gratitude

Also write in your journal at least three things you are grateful for. Try doing this every day for the next three months and note how the list grows and how your attitudes change.

Resources

Diana Rajchel, *Mabon: Rituals, Recipes & Lore for the Autumn Equinox* (St. Paul: Llewellyn Publications, 2015).

Ellen Dugan, *Autumn Equinox: The Enchantment of Mabon* (St. Paul: Llewellyn Publications, 2005).

Sarah Ban Breathnach, *Simple Abundance: A Daybook of Comfort and Joy* (New York: Grand Central Publishing, 2009).

Rachel Pollack, *The New Tarot Handbook: Master the Meanings of the Cards* (St. Paul: Llewellyn Publications, 2012).

Fool's Dog Tarot apps—www.foolsdog.com.

CHAPTER SEVENTEEN
Communicating with Spirits

W e've explored connecting with your Greater Self, with gods, and with nature spirits through meditation, contemplation, offerings, and ritual. Now we're going to look at ways to work with ancestral and other human spirits as well as techniques that will help you take all kinds of spirit contact deeper. We can learn to get into states of mind where much clearer communication is possible and come to an expanded awareness of the levels at which material reality is created. Techniques for reaching these states of mind are collectively called trancework.

I rather broadly define trance as tuning the mind to different levels of consciousness in order to communicate with nonphysical beings. One of those beings can be yourself—levels of your subconscious and unconscious are often best accessed through a trance state such as hypnosis. But the types of trance I'm focusing on here are about contacting gods, guides, ancestors, and other denizens of the spirit realm.

There are a lot of different flavors of trance, but they all lead to states of inner awareness that we are not normally tuned to. I like the term "non-ordinary reality" as a culturally neutral moniker for these states, which differ in tone and content from each other, depending on various cultural and metaphysical factors, but are all sourced from inner realities. They involve a shift of consciousness from the outer world to the inner.

There are many names for trance states associated with particular traditions, and essentially every religion or spiritual tradition acknowledges their transformative power. I believe that it is best to be a member—either by birth, adoption, or initiation—of any religion, culture, or tradition whose trance techniques, mythology, and iconography you use. There are those who disagree with me and believe that sufficient research and a respectful attitude are all that is required, and that may be true for experienced practitioners who are careful about cultural appropriation. But I believe that it's important to have some kind of philosophical and mythological structures in place as well as known, reliable spirit guardians while you are learning to make these trance journeys. The spirit world is vast, and it's good to have a map.

I was born and raised in Manhattan, so you can dump me anywhere in Central Park in the middle of the night and I'll find my way out without too much trouble. But someone from rural Montana could easily get turned around and end up in Harlem when their hotel's way down in Soho. (Of course, I'd be at a similar disadvantage were I dropped into the Montana mountains.) Also, at least some sections of Central Park in the middle of the night are not safe (ditto for the Montana mountains). So if you're both lost and unguarded, the likelihood of your getting mugged goes up exponentially. But if you have a team of armed guards and someone with a map and compass, then it's just an evening's walk in the park. Travels in inner space are no different, except that they need not conform to the laws of physics. And while getting mugged in inner space might not land you in the hospital immediately, it can have a pronounced effect on your life. Hence my suggestion that you have a structure for your trance journeys, a path to follow there and back, and some kind of preliminary connection with guardian spirits.

The world of non-ordinary reality is even larger and more complex than our physical world. There is no need to be afraid of it if you approach it with the same common sense as you would travel in the physical world. In this case, common sense involves getting training. In-person is best, but books like the ones I list in the resources section at the end of this chapter can help you learn to tune yourself to non-ordinary reality without getting lost or mugged.

Is there danger? Yes, some, and more for some people than others, but it can be minimized. There's danger getting in your car and driving to the grocery store. But you learned how to drive, and if you drive defensively and don't run any red lights, you'll probably be fine. Life involves a certain amount of risk, and we should always assess why we are taking risks. If you have a strong feeling that trancework isn't for you, or it isn't a good path for you to follow right now, then heed your intuition and continue to work with meditation, offerings, and ritual to connect with the spirit world.

But now let's look at why you might want to learn to achieve trance states despite any risks or difficulties.

For some of you, curiosity about what your mind can do is all the motivation you need to explore trancework, but, in my experience, most people start this work because they want a closer connection with the spirit world. For me, it was a deep desire to connect with nature spirits. Trance states allow us to communicate with beings of spirit more clearly than we can through meditation alone. This includes gods and nature spirits, of course, but trance states are also needed when we are trying to communicate with other types of spirits—our personal helping spirits in particular. These spirits can be of many different types—gods, animal and other nature spirits, teachers from other realms—but will almost invariably include the dead, the ancestors, the humans who preceded us. We'll look specifically at communicating with our ancestors in the next chapter, when we celebrate the autumn/winter midpoint, a.k.a. Samhain.

The "Why" of Trance

But there is another good reason to work with trance states, and that is to become a better magician. Magic not only requires the magician to shift their consciousness at will but is aided through the help of various spirit beings.

Meditation is one way of altering, exploring, and controlling our consciousness. Meditation, as we've practiced it so far, involves becoming aware of our thoughts, quieting our minds, developing intuition, and opening our awareness to nonphysical consciousnesses. But if we want to utilize and direct the forces of manifestation, if we want to work on the level of consciousness that directly creates our physical reality, if we want to develop deeper relationships with nonphysical consciousnesses, then it is helpful to take our minds further and explore the techniques of trancework and spirit contact.

Magic, as I've noted earlier, is an influence. If you want to become more influential, not to mention understand more about how the universe works, one of the best ways to do that is to explore trance states and work closely with spirit allies. If Consciousness is, in fact, the ground of being, the Creator, All That Is, then learning to alter the consciousness that is our own, to tune it into the levels at which the blueprints of reality are drawn, must be basic to creating change in the world.

Methods of Trance Induction

There are a limited number of ways to reliably put yourself in a trance state. While different religions and cultures have their own specific methodologies, they generally involve some form of ritual that incorporates one or more of the following trance-inducing techniques:

- Percussion
- Music
- Movement
- Vocalization (singing, chanting, toning)
- Entheogens (consciousness-altering drugs)
- Guided meditation
- Physical restrictions such as fasting, sleep deprivation, immobilization, or taking and holding specific body postures
- Using particular breathing patterns

Though it's best to work with a teacher, it's quite possible that you'll be working alone as you explore trance states; and since nobody's watching, you may think you can skip the preliminary ritual part and jump right into a trance induction. Don't. Ritual sets up an energetic pattern that helps direct your trance in positive, useful ways. Please don't get your back up over the idea of ritual. I mentioned this earlier, but it's worth repeating because I've found that it's a difficult prejudice for some people to get over.

If you're one of them, think of it this way. If I'm going to ride a horse, I don't just walk into the barn and jump on the horse. If I want to ride, there is an entire ritual I go through that involves dressing in appropriate clothing, brushing the horse, picking out its feet, putting on the bridle, saddle pad, and saddle, and rechecking the girth just before I mount. While I'm doing all this,

I'm talking to and stroking the horse, communicating through voice, touch, and resonance. This ritual clues the horse in to the plan and creates the necessary physical structures and mindset for a safe and comfortable experience for both horse and rider. Think of your subconscious as the horse. The ritual helps you prepare to take a trip into other realms of consciousness.

As far as techniques go, I recommend starting simply, with percussion, music, mantra (repeated prayer), or guided meditations. Many of the books listed in the resources section of this chapter give instruction on how to achieve trance safely and effectively using one or more of these techniques. While I think that entheogens (consciousness-altering drugs used for religious or spiritual purposes, such as ayahuasca and peyote) can be very helpful in our spiritual explorations, I would suggest developing good control over your own mind though meditation and trance before trying them. You will also need to travel somewhere they are legal, and I also *strongly* recommend working with a teacher who has considerable experience and preferably a cultural background in their use. While they may be helpful and interesting, they are not at all necessary, and can be dangerous if misused.

In addition to different techniques, there are also different types of trance. Types of trance are classified on the intent more than the technique. Here's a brief overview of the main ones.

Divine embodiment is an umbrella term for allowing a deity to speak through you to others. This can range from a light trance state where you are at least somewhat aware of what's going on, to full possessory trance, as is practiced in Vodoun, where participants are "ridden" by one of the loa (tutelary spirits/deities of Vodoun), often with remarkable physical manifestations and interactions with other participants in the ritual. (This is one of those kinds of trance states you definitely don't want to try at home. Get training and initiation first.)

Channeling is similar to divine embodiment, but the channel speaks for spirits who are generally not deities. There is rarely ritual involved and few or no physical manifestations (though changes in the channel's voice and facial expressions are common). There is the same range of trance depth as in divine embodiment—from speaking while still conscious of your surroundings to a full possession, where the spirit is allowed to fully take over the voice and body of the channel, who will usually remember nothing of what occurred during the trance. Approach this kind of work with caution, and preferably with an experienced teacher who can determine if the spirit coming through is wise and benevolent or someone you really don't want hanging around, and then banish it if needed.

Mediumship is similar to channeling, but the word is usually used more to denote those who communicate with the dead.

Divinatory trance, as you have probably already concluded, is a type of trance that is used to divine what is removed from the person in time and/or space. This includes prediction, remote viewing, prophecy, etc. There are different ways of going about this, some involving spirit contact, others simply reaching a different state of awareness, like getting a bird's-eye view from outside time and space.

Pathworking and *shamanic journey* are similar in that they both use active imagination. The main difference is that pathworking generally has a specific map that you follow with a description of the territory, whereas shamanic journey allows the unconscious—usually with the help of a spirit or spirits—to provide both the map and the territory. Both of these types of trance rely on the ability to imagine different surroundings, and that generally relies heavily on visualization.

You will often hear people who offer guided meditations/pathworkings (myself included) say something like, "Don't worry if you can't visualize, just follow along with what I'm saying like you were reading a book and imagining what was going on in the book." And I think one can have transformative meditations with minimal visualization.

But, unless you have developed other senses to an exceptional degree, it is likely that sight is your primary way of perceiving your surroundings. Which means that working to improve your visualization skills—and there are ways of doing that, as you will learn through your reading—can improve both your divinatory and magical skills.

The Bad Guys and How To Avoid Them

I am often asked if trancework might attract malevolent or parasitic spirits or trigger psychotic episodes in those who are vulnerable, for whatever reason. My answer is always a qualified yes to both of these questions. Yes, because trancework can light you up on the inner planes, so you become more noticeable to those whose vision is tuned to those planes. The yes is qualified because if you do the work with care and the guidance of an established system, and the teachers and/or guiding spirits within that system, certain protections will be built in. I strongly suggest starting with proven protocols for trance induction and journey. You can develop your own techniques once you've gained experience travelling in other realms.

I should also point out that some people attract problematic spirits and can be triggered into psychotic episodes by spirits even if they don't do trancework. You might be surprised to discover how many psychotic episodes are, in fact, at least partially caused by spirits, either deliberately or simply by proximity, and how many runs of ill-health or seemingly bad "luck" can be traced to spirit influences on our subtle bodies. Those who have made a study of trancework learn to discern these kinds of problems, which can happen to anyone, and know what their options are to banish and heal.

It's important to note that spirits, like humans, animals, and other physical beings, are not always helpful and beneficent. In fact, they can be problematic and occasionally downright evil. But before you start shaking in your boots, remember two things. First, the universe bends toward love. There are plenty of spirits who are beneficent, protective, and influence the ambient energies of a person or place. Second, just as you lock your doors, don't walk through high-crime areas alone at night, and avoid telling your secrets to the office gossip, it's not that difficult to protect yourself against harmful spirits.

Regular meditation, energy work such as cleansing, grounding, and centering, and developing relationships with personal guides and gods will go a long way toward keeping you safe and spiritually clear. Develop some kind of daily practice that affirms your connection to your guides and to your spiritual path. Most of the books listed in this chapter's resource section will help you do that.

The clergy, elders, or wise ones of most religions and spiritual/magical paths are usually trained to be aware of spirit intrusions and clear them, so if you feel as though you are having problems that can be traced to otherworldly influences, a visit to a spiritual practitioner who comes well-recommended can be helpful as well. But be careful not to give your power away to another. There are a remarkable number of well-meaning idiots as well as outright frauds who purport to give spiritual guidance and clear malefic influences. Do your due diligence, trust your gut, and never be afraid to get a second opinion. Read some of these books to learn how to develop your own daily practice of spiritual cleansing, connection, and blessing.

Now that we've explored communicating with spirits, we'll move on to the spookiest time of the year and look at how we can commune with the spirits of those who were once human—our ancestors and beloved dead.

Resources

Diana Paxson, *Trance-portation: Learning to Navigate the Inner World* (Newburyport: Weiser Books, 2008).

Janet Farrar and Gavin Bone, *Lifting the Veil: A Witches' Guide to Trance-Prophesy, Drawing Down the Moon, and Ecstatic Ritual* (Portland: Acorn Guild Press, 2016).

Ivo Dominguez, Jr., *Spirit Speak: Knowing and Understanding Spirit Guides, Ancestors, Ghosts, Angels, and the Divine* (Newburyport: Weiser Books, 2008).

Dolores Ashcroft-Nowicki, *Highways of the Mind: The Art and History of Pathworking* (Sechelt: Twin Eagles Publishing, 2011).

Bradford Keeney, Ph.D., *Shaking Medicine: The Healing Power of Ecstatic Movement* (Merrimac: Destiny Books, 2007).

Sandra Ingerman, *Shamanic Journeying: A Beginner's Guide* (Boulder: Sounds True, 2008).

Swami Sivananda Radha, *Mantras: Words of Power* (Kootenay: Timeless Books, 2011).

Jason Miller, *Protection and Reversal Magick* (Newburyport: Weiser Books, 2006).

CHAPTER EIGHTEEN
Samhain—The Autumn/ Winter Midpoint

F inally, we come to the autumn/winter midpoint, the most well-known of the Wiccan Sabbats—Samhain. Traditionally celebrated on October 31/November 1, the astronomical date is right around November 7. As I often do with the cross-quarters, when the traditional dates are usually offset by a few days from the astronomical one, I start celebrating on October 31 and keep on going for a week.

In the Gaelic lands, particularly Ireland and Scotland, there is evidence that celebrations at this time of year date back millennia. The celebration was Christianized in the ninth century as All Saints/All Hallows/All Souls Days, and the Irish brought their customs for these days—which included things like masks, lanterns carved from turnips, divination, offerings to and honoring of the dead—to America during the Great Famine migrations of the mid-nineteenth century. And so the great modern festival of ghosts, skeletons, witches, and candy consumption, Halloween, was born.

Samhain marks the end of summer. In the agricultural calendar, it is the time when the herds are brought down from summer pastures. Then decisions must be made about which animals to slaughter and preserve for food and which to keep fed and sheltered through the winter. Like Beltane, it is a time when the veil between the worlds is considered to be thin, but now, instead of a focus on growth and the living, the focus is on death and the dead. The Fae are thought to be particularly active in our world at both these times as well.

There's an essay in Patricia Monaghan's *Seasons of the Witch* that I always read at the beginning of my Samhain ritual because it sets the tone for the season so well. She begins by noting that the harvest is in, and that is a reason for celebration. But then she gets to the heart of the season, recognizing that:

> ... nothing more is growing. Nothing more will grow this year. There will never be more than there is now. And the winds of autumn descend to tear seed from stalk, to scatter what has not been captured ...

> Such communion! As we pick the pumpkin from its shriveled stalk, as we press the juice from apple's flesh, as we tear out carrot life by its roots, we taste the deepest knowledge we can have: we need others to survive. That we breathe only because something has died. That we make our own flesh of the flesh of the world.[15]

This beginning to the ritual (and I urge you to get the book and read the entire essay) helps us acknowledge, within the transformative container of ritual, how inextricably life and death are intertwined in our world. The work of this time is to understand that we cannot fully celebrate life without also celebrating death's part in our worldly dance.

There are a number of ways to ritually observe this time of year. We can take an assessment of our lives and, over the next six weeks or so, sort the wheat from the chaff. Decide what to leave behind in the old year and allow it to die with the frost. Acknowledge what we have and what we will keep and cherish through the winter.

Another profound way of working with this time of year is to face death. On a personal level, this means considering your own death. What do you believe will happen when you die? What will you leave behind? If you get to review your life after you're dead, how do you think you'll feel about how you lived it?

This is also a good time to honor your ancestors of blood and bone—those whose DNA led to you as the result. Veneration of the dead is widespread, even in modern times, from the saints of Catholicism to Asian and African

---

15. Patricia Monaghan, *Seasons of the Witch* (Oak Park: Delphi Press, 1992), 65.

ancestral customs. But modern Westernized cultures mostly ignore the dead, much to our detriment. Most ancestor-venerating cultures considered the dead to have powers within this world for both good and evil and a particular interest in their descendants.

There are cultures who believe that the dead cannot take their place as an ancestor unless and until they are recognized as such by the living. They believe that our modern lack of respect for our ancestors has resulted in crowds of restless and unsettled spirits of the dead who remain close by, interfering with the living, to our detriment. There are cultures who believe that only some of the dead have the wisdom and awareness to become ancestors, those to whom one can turn for advice and help. Other cultures simply revere all of their ancestors.

There are also varying beliefs about what happens after death, and you have some thinking to do about what you believe. The books below will give you some ideas, but one particular idea we should consider here is the concept of reincarnation. It is a widespread belief, and unlike many of our beliefs about death and the dead, this one has a remarkable amount of evidence to support it. Much of it is anecdotal, but there has been serious research done, and the results are compelling.

The Case for Reincarnation

Before we get into communicating with the dead, let's consider the concept of reincarnation, the notion that a person's consciousness can survive death, because it raises some questions that require answers if we want to connect with specific ancestral or other once-human spirits.

There is some interesting research on the topic of reincarnation, and the results of that research, along with the sheer amount of well-documented anecdotal evidence, should have scientists scrambling for their grant applications. I'm sure one reason this kind of research is not pursued more vigorously is because if it turns out that consciousness survives the death of the body and can be reborn in a new body with accurate memories of the previous lifetime, then the entire foundation on which our science rests must be revisited, and probably rebuilt from the ground up.

The concept of reincarnation causes a lot of trouble for people who are used to thinking in a linear fashion. "If my Aunt Fanny is dead and I try to contact her as an ancestral spirit, but she's reincarnated, how can she respond?" is a common question. Keep in mind that each of us has an Oversoul, a Greater Self, and while she may have reincarnated in any one of seven billion or so guises, her life as Aunt Fanny still exists within a particular stream of Consciousness, of time and space.

Our Greater Self is far larger than we realize—than we can even comprehend from our current perspective—and we have an existence outside of the linearity and limits of time and space. Aunt Fanny and the person she is in her current incarnation are different expressions of the same Greater Self. Different incarnations are not generally aware of each other, at least once they reach age seven or so, because their physical existences are in different times and places, and it would be counter-productive as adults to remember our previous lives. But as you'll see if you do some reading, children often remember exact, checkable details about their previous lives, even when there is no other connection between those two lives. But then, as we grow, we forget—as we are meant to. Our explorations in consciousness here in time and space go best, for the most part, if we stay focused in *our* time and space.

My sense of this is that our Greater Self holds all of our incarnations in an eternal, timeless reality and at least some of those incarnations maintain individual awareness when they transition out of their own time and space into a larger reality, where they are aware of Earth and its denizens to some extent and interact to some extent. I believe this depends on the individual—some may choose to stick around for a while, albeit in another dimension, and others move right on to different realms of Consciousness and creativity.

Some spirits are more connected to us in our current incarnation than others. Here's an example. Back in 2007, I went through a five-day ancestralization process guided by Malidoma Somé, author and elder of the Dagara tribe of west Africa. The Dagara revere and communicate with their ancestors, and this process, culminating in an all-night ceremonial vigil, was based in Dagaran protocols and designed to connect the participants, all of whom were raised in modern Western cultures, to their ancestral lines.

My father had died the year before, and I expected that I might make contact with him. But it was my mother, who had died in 1975, whose presence I felt strongly and with whom I communed in my meditations during the ceremony. Now, I was pretty certain that my mother had reincarnated by that time, but the part of her Greater Self who was born as Eleanor French and lived in the twentieth century, still existed. That she was still aware and developing on some level was made clear to me when I was sitting at my computer a few weeks after the ceremony and clearly heard her say in my mind, "Google me." Obviously, she is keeping up with the times!

I did Google her, and discovered that someone had posted a short film, made in the late thirties or early forties, that was a very early example of what we now call a music video. (Mom had a career as a singer in the thirties and forties.) The song was "I'm Just Wild About Harry" and the film included a scene of a car exploding. (No, really! It's on YouTube. See for yourself.) The humorous expression on her face in that scene was so familiar to me, and seeing it again affected me deeply. I came to understand that on some level she was still aware of me, that we still had a relationship, a connection, that transcended time.

Again, it can be hard for us, stuck in linear time with a sense of self that is often dependent on a separate body, to fully understand the various ramifications and differentiations of Consciousness. You'll want to do your own thinking and research, of course, and make your own decisions. But I'm going to assume that reincarnation is a thing as we move ahead. You may find that a big stretch for your imagination, but I suggest reading a couple of the books I recommend on the subject before you make up your mind one way or another.

Connecting with Your Ancestors

Ancestors give the reincarnating soul a path back through history, a tie to the human story, an anchor within time and space. Your soul may or may not have been involved with this particular bloodline in previous lives, but DNA gives you full membership in the family. Advances in epigenetics (the study of inherited changes that do not involve the DNA directly) have made it very clear that our blood ancestors' experiences affect our lives as well.

It's important to consider that not all ancestors are able to give you help or advice. Especially the more recently dead may be still acquainting themselves with reality on the other side and be a bit stuck or confused. They may make themselves known to you in one way or another, often at that liminal time between sleep and waking, as a voice you hear, or someone sitting on your bed, or a touch you barely feel. Wish them well, and if there is something you want to say to them, say it, as long as it is focused on releasing, not keeping you bound to each other, either through love or less pleasant emotions.

Helping them find their way on the other side is not your job—there are others who do that work (though you may eventually choose to take on that work yourself, when you have more experience working with spirits and the dead). You can and should honor the lives of your beloved dead in some way, but you want to call to and communicate with the ancestors who are in a place of perspective and power for help and advice. These ancestors have reviewed their own lives and are consciously working to help their descendants heal from old, ancestral wounds. They will work with you to heal inherited, ancestral pain and develop into the full promise of this lifetime.

Keep it well in mind that you are neither a victim nor a puppet. Your connection with your ancestors is a respectful, co-creative venture, that can be of considerable help to you. As you heal yourself, you heal long-standing wounds in your ancestral lines as well. So your ancestors have more than just a compassionate interest in helping you.

One of the best ways to both honor your dead and keep the lines of communication to your ancestors open is to keep an ancestor altar. The altar may be items you keep in a box that you bring out only when you are actively working with them. Others might want to have a few framed photos and perhaps some heirloom items on a table in the living room that doesn't look like an altar when you aren't working with it. If you have space/privacy, you can set up an altar where offerings can be regularly maintained, even if that's just a small space on a bookshelf.

What goes on the altar (or in the box) is an individual choice. You'll definitely want some connection with your ancestors of blood—both parental lines. You can use old photos, heirloom items, or you can get some modeling clay and make a bowl (for your mother's line) and an obelisk (for your father's line). They can be quite small. You might want to put a drop of your blood on each one, because blood calls to blood through time, space, and dimensions. If you are adopted and have no knowledge of your birth parents, you can just use the clay bowl and obelisk to represent the ancestors of your blood. You can also include ancestors of your adopted family on this altar.

If you have ancestors of spirit, lineage, or friendship to whom you feel strongly connected, by all means, include items that represent them as well if you feel so inclined. Ancestors of the land you live on, of the arts you practice, of your spiritual background—all these folks can eventually be included on your altar.

But to begin, if you've never set up an ancestral altar before, call on the ancestors of your blood. Because healing in physical reality resonates back through the ancestral bloodline, these ancestors are invested in you and your healing, and most of them will be protective of you. Yes, even the ones who were total jackasses in life gain some perspective once they reach the realm of the ancestors. But note this—you do not have to, nor should you, include any ancestors you are not at peace with. You need not honor those who did not honor you.

The only thing that must be true of all of them is that they are dead. Do *not* include photos or other representations of living people on the ancestor altar. This altar is the home of the dead. Including a picture of a living person on an altar for the dead could have a negative effect on that person.

We face death in this season, and we have a choice to shrink away in fear or open ourselves to the certainty that we will all, one day, join our ancestors. We can learn more about death's mysteries and, having faced our fears, move beyond them.

⊣ TOUCH THE EARTH ⊢

Observing

As always, go outside. Check where Sun is rising and setting and look at what's going on in the natural world around where you live and work.

Update Your Main Altar

I hope you've been able to set up some kind of permanent altar space for yourself by now. I like to change the items and decorations on the altar at each Station on the Wheel of the Year. I find that helps me stay in tune with the changing seasons. You might want to give it a try. Usually, I switch things around at the New or Full Moon prior to the date of the Station.

Create an Ancestor Altar

Do a ritual to set up your ancestor altar. (Because ancestors tend to be fairly active spirits, I suggest not putting this altar where you sleep. Also, you may want to have a way to cover or close a door on it.) Here's one example of how that can happen.

First, do everything necessary to make sure you are not disturbed during your rite. You want to be able to go into a light trance or meditative state during the ritual, so this is important. Gather the items you have chosen to put on this altar. This should include offerings. Have ancestral items and/or your bowl and obelisk and any decorative elements you wish. For this ritual, I suggest you have offerings of either some kind of grain or ash from a sacred fire for Earth, a bowl of Water, a small votive candle (preferably red) for Fire, and some incense for Air. A small votive candle, and some incense. You should also have a drum or rattle. (If you don't have either, you can put un-popped popcorn in a small plastic pill bottle.)

Set the atmosphere, perhaps with music or natural sounds (soft, in the background) and light any candles except the votive/tea light you are using as an offering. Cleanse the space energetically in whatever way you normally work. If you are accustomed to using salt and water, I'd suggest replacing that with a tea of some kind of cleansing herb, such as rosemary, rather than salt for this working.

Set up your altar in any way that feels appropriate to you. The directions associated with the dead and the ancestors are the south (in the West African Dagara and Hindu traditions), the west (in Celtic/European and some Native American traditions), and the north (some Native American and northern Pagan traditions). I don't know of any traditions that use the east as the place of the dead, but they may well exist.

Place the photos, and/or heirloom items, and/or bowl and obelisk on the altar. You may want to put a cloth down first, or a special tile of some kind. (You can also use other decorations, but if they are placed on this altar to honor the dead in the ritual, then they belong to the dead. They are no longer yours.) Then place the offerings, but without lighting the incense or candle.

Ground and center yourself and enter a light trance state. If you don't feel comfortable with entering trance yet, just focus on your breath, bring your mind into the present moment, and sit with that awareness for a bit.

Now pick up the candle and hold it up in a gesture of offering, state that you are offering this candle and its light to your ancestors, and with that intent light the candle. Do the same with the incense, the bowl or glass of water, and the grain or ash. (If the altar is a private, permanent one, you might want to scatter the ash or grain across it. You can also just leave it in a small offering bowl.)

Pick up your drum or rattle and begin a simple rhythm. You don't need to get fancy—just a simple, heartbeat rhythm will get the attention of the ancestors. You can also just pound your hand on the ground, as the Dagara do—and that has the advantage of being something you can do just about anywhere when you want to call your ancestors.

Once you have a rhythm established, call upon your ancestors. You can do that just by talking with them about your intention for this ritual and your desire to work more closely with them (yes, out loud), or you can say something like this:

I call upon those ancestors of mine who are established in the ancestral realm. The ones who have the vision, perspective, clarity, and wisdom needed to advise me, your descendant. I ask that you join me here and aid me in creating a place for you within my world, within my home, where we can commune and learn together. Where we can share what can be shared across the veil between the world of the dead and the world of the living, creating healing for both.

I offer you here incense and candle, water and ash [or grain; if you are giving other offerings, mention them here as well]. Please accept these offerings in the spirit of family, love, and connection with which they are given. I dedicate this altar to my ancestors and ask you to take your place in the realm of the ancestors so that you may guide and protect me [or us, if you have children; mention their names here—you can include your spouse, but ideally, they should have their own ancestral practice, and yes, you can have a combined family ancestral altar if you want].

Now, just spend some time talking with your ancestors. Let them know what your life is like. Tell them what you are grateful for and what you struggle with. Tell them where you want your life to go, what kind of person you want to be, and ask them to guide you. Keep the percussion going softly as you speak, and then spend some silent time listening.

When you feel the time is right and your communication is complete for now, thank the ancestors for their presence and blessings and blow out the candle. I usually see the vortex of energy that forms around the altar like a camera lens that opens fully when in ritual and shuts down to a small opening attached to the altar when the ritual is over. You might also visualize a gate on the altar that shuts at the end of the ritual. Use one of these or a similar visualization to return the space and your head to normal physical reality and indicate to the ancestors that they should now return to their realm.

Bring yourself out of your trance state in whatever way you normally do (clapping three times and touching the ground with that intention works fine), then spend a few minutes journaling about your experience if you want. When you are done, ground and center, then close sacred space in whatever way you do that.

And that's it! For now. You've started a relationship and, as with any relationship, it's important that you hold up your end. So come back to your altar regularly. You don't need to repeat the whole ritual, just give fresh offerings. Get in the habit of telling your ancestors what's going on, asking for their guidance, and paying attention when that guidance comes in the form of synchronicities or intuition.

⊣ KISS THE SKY ⊢

Hit the Books

Do some reading about reincarnation, near-death experiences, and different religious and cultural beliefs about death.

Explore Your Beliefs

Spend some time thinking and journaling about death. Do you believe in reincarnation, in the survival of individual consciousness after death? Are you afraid of dying? Why or why not?

Plan for Your Own Death

Make sure you have a will and health care power of attorney in place. One thing everyone can agree on is that death can happen in an instant, even to young people.

Resources

Diana Rajchel, *Samhain: Rituals, Recipes & Lore for Halloween* (St. Paul: Llewellyn Publications, 2015).

Sylvia Cranston, *Reincarnation: The Phoenix Fire Mystery: An East-West Dialogue on Death and Rebirth from the Worlds of Religion, Science, Psychology, Philosophy* (Pasadena: Theosophical University Press, 1998).

Jim B. Tucker, M.D., *Life Before Life: Children's Memories of Previous Lives* (New York: St. Martin's Griffin Press, 2008).

Michael Newton, *Journey of Souls: Case Studies of Life Between Lives* (St. Paul: Llewellyn Publications, 1994).

Ian Stevenson, M.D., *Children Who Remember Previous Lives: A Question of Reincarnation* (Jefferson: McFarland Press, 2000).

Chris Carter, *Science and the Afterlife Experience: Evidence for the Immortality of Consciousness* (Rochester: Inner Traditions, 2012).

Raven Grimassi, *Communing with the Ancestors: Your Spirit Guides, Bloodline Allies, and the Cycle of Reincarnation* (Newburyport: Weiser Books, 2016).

Malidoma Somé, *The Healing Wisdom of Africa* (New York: TarcherPerigee, 1999).

Padma Sambhava, Robert Thurman (Tr.), *The Tibetan Book of the Dead: Liberation Through Understanding in the Between* (New York: Bantam Books, 1993).

Christopher Penczak, *The Mighty Dead* (Salem: Copper Cauldron Publishing, 2013).

CHAPTER NINETEEN
Finding Your Path

N ow the Wheel of the Year spirals back to the Yuletide season, to another Winter Solstice. I hope this book has helped you clarify your thoughts and feelings about spirituality, magic, and the remarkable reality that lies beyond the rather dreary dictates and limitations of purely materialistic science. If you've done at least some of the work in this book, you should feel better equipped to explore spiritual realities using the tools of meditation, ritual, trancework, and magic.

Science itself, of course, is not dreary at all, and hopefully you've also gained insights into the current state of science by reading some of the books I recommended. Both science and spirituality are attempts to discover and understand how the world works and how to best live in it. Both are driven by a search for truth, and I am convinced that both paths to knowledge intersect in a single truth.

If you are a seeker of truth, then both science and spirituality should be of interest to you. As we pursue these interests, the deeper and wider our inquiries go, the more we realize just how large and complex reality is and how little we really know. This can be scary and disconcerting, but we won't uncover many truths if we won't face our fears because then we'll refuse to see what's right in front of us. It's a fact that we will never, ever, understand it all. We can only comprehend a small portion of just our physical universe, much less Consciousness. Some people find that frightening. I find it comforting, but only because I believe that the universe turns toward love, and I'm thrilled that there will always be more to discover.

Wakan Tanka is a term used by the Lakota to describe the Creator, or the ultimate spiritual force. It is often translated as "Great Spirit," but Lakota writer and activist Russell Means noted in his autobiography that the words are better translated as "Great Mystery." I like that term. It seems to me to be the most accurate description we can give of the source and destination of our existence.

The Great Mystery will always be a mystery to us. Consciousness encompasses and transcends our physical world and so cannot be understood from within its confines. But our attempts to solve the Great Mystery—to come to a greater understanding of how the reality we experience is created and how we ourselves have agency in that creation—are no less important because the Great Mystery is impossible to solve. That deep need to understand, to know more, seems to be built into the human spirit. We are clearly meant to solve smaller mysteries that lead us closer to the greater one.

Our pursuit of knowledge through an exploration of spiritual realities should lead to an expanded understanding of physical realities as well because they are not separate. Both are part of our human experience. But, most importantly, ongoing exploration of spiritual realities will help us decide how we should live within the physical world we wake up to every morning and what we should do with the expanded understanding of reality our search for truth brings us. It will help us make wiser choices that lead to a better world for us all.

Many people practice meditation and other esoteric technologies in pursuit of spiritual enlightenment or awakening—the full recognition of the individual's oneness with Consciousness. And this is certainly a valid and highly desirable outcome. But it cannot stand alone. Since you've gotten this far in the book, I expect that you are one of those who believe that if a spiritual path is to be valid for you, it must "grow corn." In other words, it must lead to practical, positive effects in your everyday life and that of your family and friends, not just give you an expanded awareness of the reality of Consciousness behind the illusion of time and space.

Modern science certainly does grow corn. Lots of it. But that corn is grown—both literally and figuratively—in ways that we know now, without a doubt, are unsustainable for future generations. Modern science, for all its successes, has carelessly sown seeds that destroy ecosystems, strip irreplaceable resources, and steal the resources of the planet from our descendants. Science is long overdue for a radical shift in perspective and vision because far too many of the major players of mainstream culture—which includes scientists, politicians, economists, and business power players—have demonstrated that they have limited vision and little care for the future.

The climate is changing drastically, as predicted. The flooding is happening. The water is poisoned or gone in many places. Critical resources are becoming scarce. People are suffering, starving, and ill all over the world. We are, as always, at war. Yes, we have smartphones, and some of us live lives of extreme comfort with plentiful food, clothing, shelter, and entertainment. But that comfort—aside from the fact that it is not shared with the majority of the world's population, many of who live lives of extreme poverty—will be short-lived for everyone if we do not come to understand that we live in an interconnected world. If we continue to ignore those connections and refuse to understand that we cannot destroy the natural world with impunity, then civilization will die as the Web of Life is shredded.

This is where spiritual awareness comes in. There is a difference between understanding the math behind quantum non-locality and the visceral awareness, gained through spiritual inquiry, of the forces that join us all together within the Web of Life. I believe that we must come to fully understand our interconnectedness with everything in the universe, as well as the primacy and power of Consciousness, on levels far more experiential and complex than just an intellectual one if we are to survive. We must feel and sense our way into a larger reality if we want to change reality. We must learn to follow our hearts as well as our minds.

Science is a telescope and a microscope, a way of looking at the world that helps us grasp how it works so we can change it to our benefit. It is a fine way of discovering, classifying, and codifying the reality we experience in ways that bring progress. It leads us to invent equipment and machinery that help us discern the workings of the world and make our lives easier. But magnification alone does not bring knowledge or wisdom. You have to point the telescope in the right direction, and put the right objects under the microscope. The scientific method, as a system of thinking, a way of approaching a question, is a fine tool for learning about the world and accumulating a body of knowledge. But it is not the only way, nor is it the ultimate arbiter of truth.

It is certainly no arbiter of morality, and informed ethics are foundational to any lasting civilization.

Our logical, rational minds are simply unable to fully grasp the totality of even the physical universe, much less the fullness of Consciousness. And yet, we are, always and forever, an integral part of that Consciousness. The knowledge that we can work with the powers of our own consciousness, combined with the powers of Nature and spirit, can lead to an integration of spirit and science that changes our lives and helps change the world around us. Knowing that Consciousness is creative and that we are co-creators leads to more aware, thoughtful creation as we learn what is possible.

Spiritual and personal growth rarely happen in a single stunning moment of enlightenment. For most people, awareness grows in mysterious, creative ways, arising from a combination of reasoned thought, intuitive insight, increased awareness, and received wisdom. It comes with the gradual shedding of fears and is accompanied by an increase in curiosity. It comes with the elimination of judgmental attitudes and the growth of discernment, with the release of fantasies of control in exchange for stepping into the true power of self-knowledge and an ever-expanding awareness of the universe and our creative abilities within it, both as individuals and en masse. It comes with understanding the true nature of our connections to each other and to the world around us.

I hope by now you have an altar, a journal, and have met with at least one or two of your guides and gods. Perhaps you've done a ritual or two and even established a daily practice that helps you stay connected to spiritual realities. Now what will you do? There is power in this work, and with power comes responsibility. Not because I say that it's so, but because gaining power requires taking responsibility for your own experiences. This does not mean you brought every bad thing that happens to you on yourself. But you chose to come into this life knowing that it would be a challenge. I hope you will live up to that challenge and walk the path your soul has laid out for you with courage and conviction.

Doing spiritual work, practicing magic, leads to a broadening of creative abilities, and the flowering of creativity inevitably brings a vision of what can be. Can you hold a vision for yourself and for Earth and the Web of Life? Can you see beyond current problems and limitations of our world to a better way of living in the world? To find that vision and hold it, to manifest it, requires more than just intellectual reasoning. It requires experience, and experience comes through doing the work.

I'll leave you with a quote from Jane Roberts's Seth that has been a spiritual touchstone for me for many years.

> Your spirit joined itself with flesh, and in flesh, to experience a world of incredible richness, to help create a dimension of reality of colors and of form. Your spirit was born in flesh to enrich a marvelous area of sense awareness, to feel energy made into corporeal form.
>
> You are here to use, enjoy, and express yourself through the body. You are here to aid in the great expansion of consciousness.
>
> You are not here to cry about the miseries of the human condition, but to change them when you find them not to your liking through the joy, strength and vitality that is within you; to create the spirit as faithfully and beautifully as you can in flesh.[16]

Adventures await you. Blessings on your journey.

---

16. Jane Roberts, *The Nature of Personal Reality* (San Rafael: Amber Allen Publishing, 1994) Session 615.

Index

To Write to the Author

If you wish to contact the author or would like more information about this book, please write to the author in care of Llewellyn Worldwide Ltd. and we will forward your request. Both the author and the publisher appreciate hearing from you and learning of your enjoyment of this book and how it has helped you. Llewellyn Worldwide Ltd. cannot guarantee that every letter written to the author can be answered, but all will be forwarded. Please write to:

Diotima Mantineia
℅ Llewellyn Worldwide
2143 Wooddale Drive
Woodbury, MN 55125-2989
Please enclose a self-addressed stamped envelope for reply,
or $1.00 to cover costs. If outside the U.S.A., enclose
an international postal reply coupon.

Many of Llewellyn's authors have websites with additional information and resources. For more information, please visit our website at http://www.llewellyn.com.